# Statecraft and Society in China

## Chinese grassroots politics

中国社会政经方略

**Edition 2022 - Frans Vandenbosch**

# China



## Grassroots Politics

| | | |
|---|---|---|
| 中 | Zhōng | China's |
| 国 | guó | |
| 社 | shè | social |
| 会 | huì | |
| 政 | zhèng | political |
| 经 | jīng | and economic |
| 方 | fāng | |
| 略 | lüè | strategy |

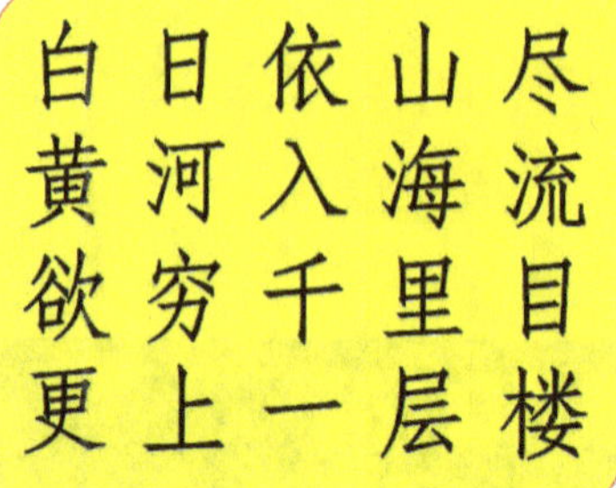


Fig. 1 The sun beyond the mountains glows.

Fig. 2 WeChat QR




Statecraft and Society in China.indd 30.03.2021
update 20.10.2022

D/2020/xxxx/xx

ISBN: 978-9-46433-732-7

# Keyword cloud:

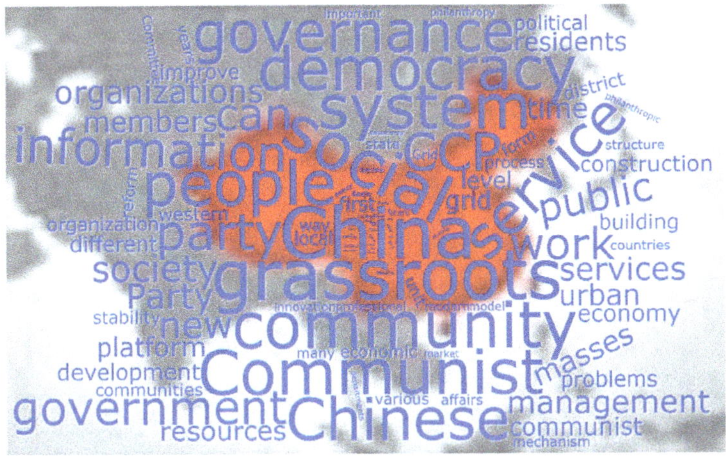


*Fig. 3 Keyword cloud*

The title of this book ***Statecraft and Society in China***
is a tribute to Cambridge professor Joseph Needham (1900 - 1995),
a fellow of the Royal Society and the British Academy, for his
life's work
***Science and Civilisation in China***.

# Table of Contents

Chengdu University Library

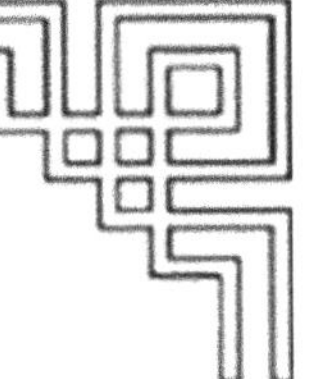

# Preface.

*#China #style #media #prejudice*

Grassroots politics in China is a topic where many are clueless and have a very different picture in mind driven by the Western Media. There are many ways they spread misinformation and mislead individuals. There's a myriad of books about top-level politics in China. Almost every week there's a new book published about Xi Jinping, his life, career and way of thinking or about Chinese politics, history, literature, language, the economy, trade, geostrategy and more. It is not too difficult to get a – often western – viewpoint on what's happening on at the top in China. Inside viewpoints, however, are somewhat rarer.

English books or reports about what's going on at Chinese grassroots level are completely non-existent. As per our Western narrative, politics is decided in Beijing and is pressed through from the top to the bottom. At a grassroots level, there are only obedient and loyal followers, kneaded by a propaganda apparatus and kept under control by a censorship machine.

This book will cut through that picture. It will break with the common assumptions; it invites the reader to take stock of a very different image of China. It will show what's really going on in China. How ordinary Chinese people engage in politics. How people's issues and concerns find their way through the system in new legislation. And how local neighbourhood committees contribute to a more harmonious society in China. It will show the unwavering, selfless commitment of thousands of Chinese people at grassroots level in local work- and in discussion groups.
This book will also show how, in the past two decades, philanthropy

with Chinese Characteristics has changed the world of
charity in China.

Some people will feel offended in reading this book. Although my
writing style might be abrasive, it is not my intention to upset my
readers. My goal for both China and the world is a harmonious
society based on correct information.

Before digging into the details of the grassroots movements in China,
a basic understanding of the Chinese political system is required.
We invite and challenge the - even occasional or chance - reader to
broaden their understanding of China as a whole and its cultural and
historical roots.

**Western mainstream media is taking us for a ride.**

Those, who do not actively gather their information from various
sources and in various languages are taken for a ride by most
Western mainstream media. Nowhere on this planet have I faced so
much misinformation, deceit and blunt propaganda as in Western
Europe. Fortunately, a growing number of conscious citizens are
gradually becoming aware of the deception by the media.

It is not too difficult for local news items to unravel the real
story behind the highly framed reporting. For news items from
neighbouring countries, it takes little effort to counter the
mainstream media's nonsense. The barriers are language and
unfamiliarity with the social or political situation in other countries.
But even then, it is hard to estimate the exact background reasons
or causes behind an incident or news item. The vast majority do not
make all these efforts and unwittingly follow the mainstream media's
explanation and framing.

For news about China, however, there are two additional hurdles to take. First, for most Westerners, there is the Chinese language, a real wall between the West and the Chinese social and regular media. The second barrier is the culture which is so different from the West. For Westerners it isn't obvious to imagine how Chinese society is organized, nor how the social norms are different from the West.

These two additional Chinese barriers are exploited in a sordid way by all of the Western media. My dissatisfaction with the Western way of reporting on China was the main reason I wrote my first book **and I owe it to the truth to refer to that issue again in this new book.**

> **Forget everything**, really everything you learned about China from the Western media.　　　　方腾波

Erase everything, really everything you've read about China in the past five decades in newspapers or seen on TV. Only with a clean slate can we explore today's China.

Wuhan Huashan Library

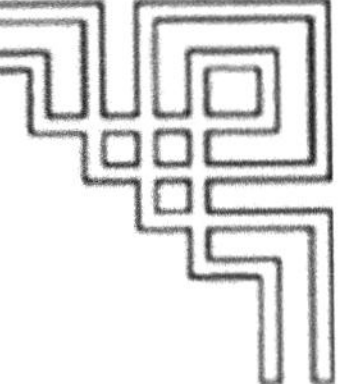



# 2.

# Introduction.

*#Sinophile #Marco-Polo #China #Europe #deterioration*

Sinophobe or Sinophile?

**Nothing has changed since Marco Polo** (1254 - 1324).

In 1271, Marco Polo went on a long journey to China with his father and uncle, arriving shortly after Kublai Khan established the Yuan dynasty. He returned to Venice 24 years later. He then dictated his book Il Milione (The Travels of Marco Polo) to Rustichello in 1296. It was the first ever realistic depiction of China. The Europeans were shocked; they couldn't believe that there was such an ancient, rich culture at the other end of the world. They regarded Marco Polo as a fantasist.

When Marco Polo was at his deathbed, he confirmed his will and got the Anointment of the Sick. The priest recommended him to take back some of his bold statements about his travels in China, to which he answered: "I have told you only half of what I know about China. The other half, I will take with me to my grave. You will not believe me anyway"

Often, I feel like Marco Polo on the day before he died.　方腾波

People have accused me of being Sinophile, who only sees the beautiful side of China. Time after time, once I have gone into the details, it appears that Sinophobes do not know the real China as it is today. We can't blame them; they're the victims of the Western mainstream media.

Europe, the old continent, is deteriorating in many ways. The economy is hardly growing; a large part of the manufacturing industry has relocated elsewhere. There are high taxes, forcing companies and scientists and individuals to move to other countries. Immigration, especially illegal immigration is casting a heavy burden on social security systems and welfare. There's the moral decline, the deterioration of education quality, the sky-high suicide rates, and the lack of hope for a better future. And finally, there is the failing political system, unwilling to understand its own civilians' needs. Care for future generations or a comprehensive long-term vision is entirely missing. Europe has not come to terms with its decline... or rather the energy is not with the Europeans. They are giving up. The west ignores China's growth at its own peril.

Europe had lost its glory long before the rise of China. The centuries of Europe's global hegemony are over. Europe is in a *relative* decline: relative because of the rising economic power of China.

There is no international anarchy; there is still an international order. Despite its problems and policy mistakes, the US remains the top dog.

But for Europe, there's no other option left. Without economic cooperation with China, Europe will gradually shrink into a meaningless continent.

And that's not just my opinion:

> Trade and economic relations between China and the EU are mutually beneficial by nature. China's opening-up will continue to provide huge opportunities for China-EU relations in the future.
> 张明大使 Ambassador Zhāng Míng, the Chinese Mission to the EU

I'm grateful to China. China and the Chinese people have treated me more than well, unexpectedly well. In China, I learned what real freedom is; I enjoyed it. In China, I learned what a government and a political system can do for their people. I had never seen that before in a Western country. I was stunned by the efficiency of the government, by the helpfulness of the police and the administration. They still know the real meaning of 'civil *servant*'.

But I hardly dare to say that back in Europe. They either don't believe me or start criticizing China. I often feel like Marco Polo on the day before he died. I feel eternal gratitude to China, serenity, but also sadness for the blindness of Europe.

If that's Sinophile, then so be it.

> There is no future for the Western economy without cooperation with China.　　　　　　　　方腾波

The Chinese Social Credit System is an important subject, closely related to the Chinese society, only very briefly mentioned in this book. This subject is so heavily polarised in the Western media with such a big gap between the Western viewpoints and Chinese reality that it is impossible to get a clear view in a few sentences. I hope to elaborate on this issue in the near future, either in separate articles or in another book.

## 致中国

我的中国，你是我年轻、永恒的爱人；

我的中国，你是我忠诚的伙伴；

我的中国，你是我的快乐源泉和命运。

是你，我的中国，给了我你的笑容；

是你，我的中国，给了我胜过我应得的。

©方腾波

Fig. 4 My China

Jingshan School Library

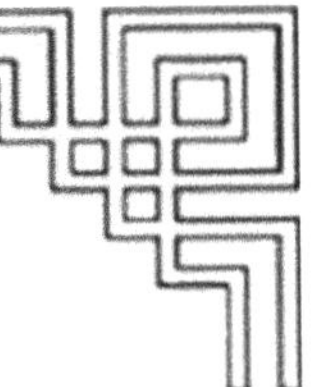



# Western Media on China.

*#media #newspeak #prejudice #truth #bias #society #truth #political-correctness*

*Biased media coverage of China, and many other countries and topics has caused anger in the masses. Over the years, more and more reliable data have confirmed what was initially only a subjective impression: media discourse is determined largely by ideological imperatives and not by reality on the ground.*

Media coverage has a lot of importance on how grassroot polititics in China is portrayed. The way our western mainstream media reports on China is disappointing, if not disgusting. The BBC, Bloomberg, CNN, the New York Times, Forbes, The Economist and The Guardian are infamously unreliable on the subject of China. They're just the tip of the iceberg. Unfortunately, many other European media outlets copy their content.

Sometimes, just sometimes, they take it too far and hit the wall:

1. **Der Spiegel Reveals Internal Fraud**[1]
   Claas Relotius , a Der Spiegel reporter, committed large-scale journalistic fraud over several years. Internal clues and research have provided significant evidence against him. He has since admitted to the falsifications and is no longer employed by **Der Spiegel**. Other media organizations may also have been affected.

2. **NRC Handelsblad** the famous Dutch newspaper fired Oscar Garschagen, their Shanghai bureau chief / correspondent in China and closed the entire NRC office in Shanghai.[2] He lived in Shanghai for over 10 years and was close to his retirement. It

---

1  Ulrich Fichtner "Der Spiegel Reveals Internal Fraud" *Spiegel Online*, 20.12.2018. http://www.spiegel.de/international/zeitgeist/claas-relotius-reporter-forgery-scandal-a-1244755.html
2  Peter Vandermeersch "NRC-correspondent Oscar Garschagen verlaat krant na journalistieke fouten" *nrc.nl*, 20.12.2017 https://www.nrc.nl/nieuws/2017/09/20/nrc-correspondent-oscar-garschagen-verlaat-krant-na-journalistieke-fouten-13094272-a1574113

was Mr. Zhang Chaochun, his news editor, who could no longer stand the falsifications and blew the whistle.

Mr Zhang collected the most striking evidence and wrote a summary entitled: *A Correspondent's Guide to Making Fake News in China*[3] for the American blog Data Insider.

Soon after, NRC Handelsblad initiated an investigation, publicly admitted the mistakes, and closed China's office.

Further details about these two cases are all over social media in both China and the West, but very rarely seen in the mainstream media. The list of similar cases is endless and fake news reporting on China is happening daily, in almost all media all over the Western hemisphere.

It is not all doom and gloom: one of the rare exceptions is the **Neue Zürcher Zeitung. (NZZ).** They still stick to sound, fact-based reporting. Where China is concerned, they're the least biased newspaper in Europe. The NZZ is also very appreciated in China. It was no coincidence that Xi Jinping published his expectations for the 2017 WEF (World Economic Forum) Davos meeting in the Neue Zürcher Zeitung in an article entitled **'Gastkommentar: «Das schönste Glück auf Erden»'**[4]

---

3  Zhang Chaoqun, "A Correspondent's Guide to Making Fake News in China" *China Data Insider*, 04.09.2017. http://www.chinadatainsider.com/index.php/2017/09/04/guide-to-making-fake-news-in-china/

4  Xi Jinping, "Das schönste Glück auf Erden" NZZ, 13.01.2017. https://www.nzz.ch/meinung/china-und-die-schweiz-die-zusammenarbeit-vertiefen-ld.139500

Switzerland was one of the first countries to establish diplomatic relations with the new China. Switzerland was the first European country to sign a Free Trade Agreement with China. Switzerland is cooperating with China in the 'One Belt, One Road' programme.

> **Forget everything**, really everything you learned about China from the Western media. 方腾波

Yiwu Grand Theatre

# 4.

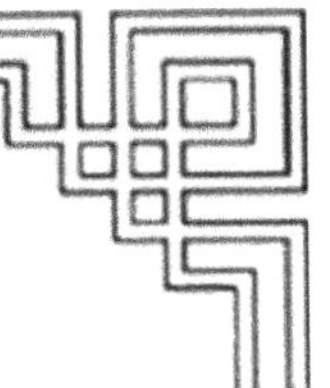

# Trust is Everything.

*#trust #guanxi #culture #society*

*China's rule of trust is what's considered an ethical rule and serves as a guide for its alliance with other countries and is what the Chinese base their relations on. The political system in China has built up this trust and hence has the highest degree of trust and future of society compared to other countries in the world.*

The chapter highlights the main factor in the success of China's political system, that is trust. Trust is everything; it is the foundation of the Chinese society.

"人而无信，不知其可也."
"How can one be acceptable without being trustworthy in words"
Confucius Analects
Chapter 2, verse 22.

Fig. 5 Confucius Analects Ch 2, Ver.22.

**There's no Christian style forgiveness in China.** In China, one can regard "When trust is broken, sorry means nothing"[5] as a hard truth. Deliberately hurting somebody's feelings or abusing trust is fatal in any relationship, whether it is private, political or business.

That same ethical rule also applies as a moral guide in China's international relationships, which should be acknowledged in our negotiations. Chinese politicians, diplomats, trade negotiators, or businessmen cannot behave in a western way in their contact with other countries. Chinese politicians will not abandon centuries of culture to adapt to Western ones and it would be unfair to expect them to do so. The Chinese 关系 guānxì system with its roots in

---

5  When trust is broken, sorry means nothing.
Frans Vandenbosch 方腾波。

Confucianism is the art of building relationships based on trust, reciprocity and mutual commitments.

**当信任已无，抱歉亦无用**
When trust is broken, sorry means nothing.　　　　方腾波

Building trust is a laborious and time-consuming process. It is not possible to speed that up or to bypass the process.

# Trust in the political system, trust in a prosperous future:

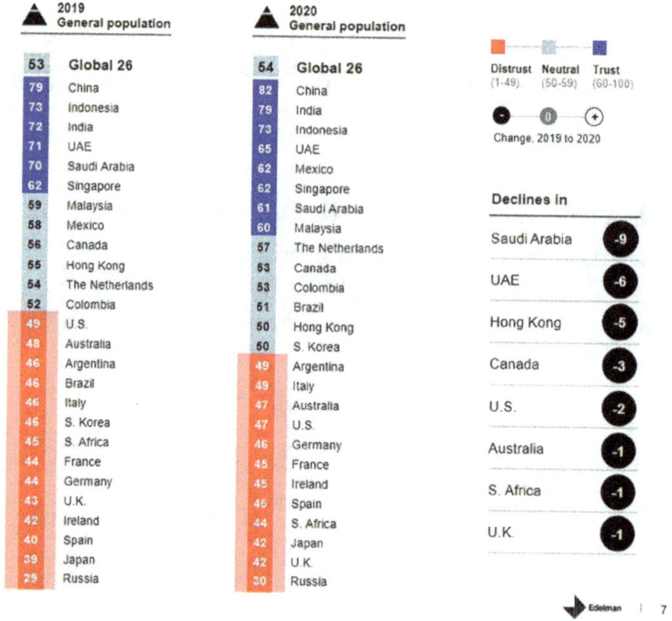

*Fig. 6 2018 Edelman Trust Barometer Global Report*

In China, the degree of trust in the political system and the future of society is the highest of the world. In the US, trust in the political system tumbled form rank 68 in 2017 to rank 45 in 2018.[6]
Also the Pew Global Survey is showing similar figures: an overwhelming majority of Chinese respondents indicated that they're satisfied with the government's handling of the economy.

---

6   Tonia E. Ries, David m. Bersoff Ph.D., Cody Armstrong, Sarah Adkins and Jamis Bruening "Edelman Trust Barometer 2018, Global Report" page 7/61, *Edelman*, 09.10.2018 https://www.edelman.com/sites/g/files/aatuss191/files/2018-10/2018_Edelman_Trust_Barometer_Global_Report_FEB.pdf

# Chinese youth have a high degree of national identity [7]

A recent survey by *China Youth Daily* revealed that 96.1 % of the respondents clearly expressed that they "often feel proud of China's accomplishments" An astonishingly high 93.5 % of the respondents said: "I would still like to be Chinese if there is a life that follows this one" And 88.6 % of the respondents stated: "No matter what happens to China, I would still stay in the country even if I have the means to leave" 82.8% of the respondents agreed with the statement "When people criticize Chinese people, I feel like they are criticizing me," and 60.1 % of respondents expressed that they "would often be embarrassed about some existing problems in the country".

On the question "How is the overall situation of China's social development since the year 1978?", 92.9 % of the youngsters held that the country is "moving in a good direction", up three percentage points when compared with results from 1998 when the same question was asked in a survey of Chinese youth carried out by the same organisation.

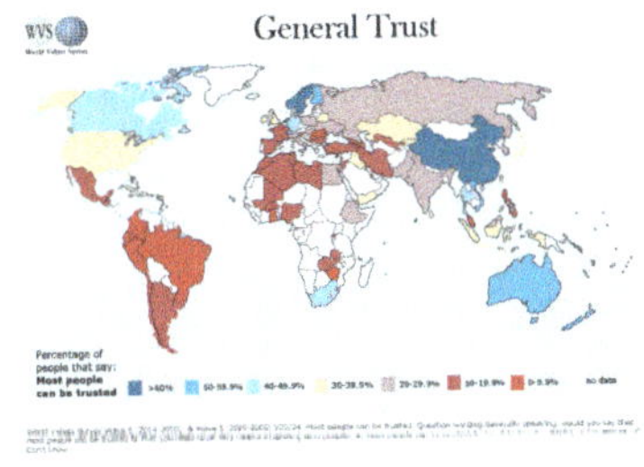

Fig. 7 People trust in other people

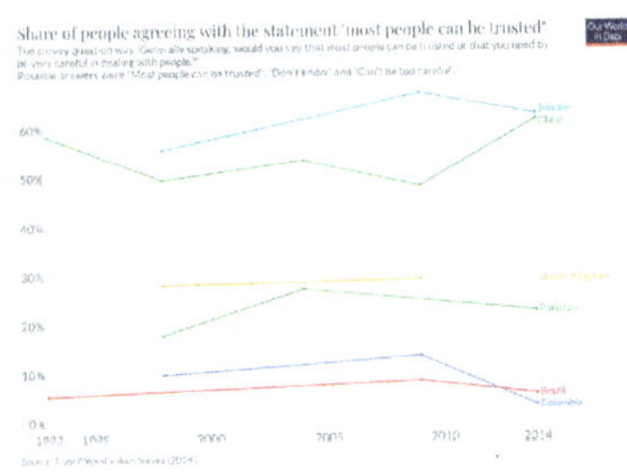

Fig. 8 Interpersonal trust

These are impressive figures, that Western countries can only dream of.

---

7  "Survey shows Chinese youth have high degree of national identity", *People's Daily Online*, 12.12.2018.
http://www.chinadaily.com.cn/a/201812/12/WS5c10709aa310eff303290883.html

Another indication of the growing self-conciousness among the youngsters in China is the flourishing Hanfu 'fashion' movement.[8] At the social media, KOC's (Key Opinion Consumers) are the important drivers to encourage the new Chinese self-awareness.

**Is China more legitimate than the West?** [9]
China is not primarily a nation-state but a civilization-state. For the Chinese, what matters is civilization. For Westerners it is nation. The most important political value in China is the integrity and unity of the civilization-state.

子曰、為政以德、譬如北辰居其所、而眾星共之。
Confucius said: To rule with virtue is like the North Star in its place, around which all other stars revolve, in homage.

---

8  "Hanfu Movement", *Wikipedia, The Free Encyclopedia*, 20.10.2019.
https://en.wikipedia.org/wiki/Hanfu_movement
9  Martin Jacques, "Is China more legitimate than the West?" *BBC Magazine*, 02.11.2012
https://www.bbc.com/news/magazine-20178655

Huiairou Liyuan Library

# 5.

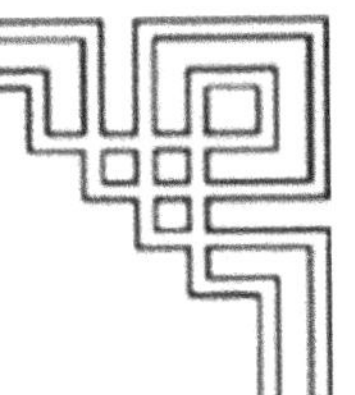

# Language, Knowledge and Truth.

*#language #knowledge #truth #society #media #newspeak
#political-correctness #bias #prejudice*

*Politics and language, the building blocks of social bonding and its conflictuality, are particularly inseparable in Chinese society. They are ubiquitous and almost inseparable in the public space: institutional debates, legal, legislative against the background of controversial definitions and denominations.*

The link between politics and language is complex and strong. It is carried in China by a socio-political, theoretical and practical lexicology. It is almost impossible to underestimate the importance of language in society and politics. Nothing, not even legislation nor propaganda is more powerful than language. Language is the glue of society, without language, there's no cohesion, no culture, no progress, no welfare.

# De Tael is gansch het Volk
(English: Language is the essence of the people)
Prudens Van Duyse (1804-1859)

Newspeak and politically correct language is suffocating our Western societies. Cathrine Gyldensted's so called 'constructive journalism' has killed the veracity and credibility of our western media.

**Confucius, 2500 years ago, was well aware of the devastating force of politically correct newspeak:**

"If language is not correct, then what is said is not what is meant; if what is said is not what is meant, then what must be done remains undone; if this remains undone, morals and art will deteriorate; if justice goes astray, the people will stand about in helpless confusion. Hence there must be no arbitrariness in what is said. This matters above everything."

**An extract of a conversation between Zilù and his Master**
(Confucius 551BC-479BC):

The Confucius Analects, Book 13, Verse 3

子路曰：衛君待子而為政，子將奚先？
子曰：必也正名乎！
子路曰：有是哉，子之迂也！奚其正？
子曰：野哉由也！君子於其所不知，蓋闕如也。名不正，則言
不順；言不順，則事不成；事不成，則禮樂不興；禮樂不興，
則刑罰不中；刑罰不中，則民無所措手足。故君子名之必可言
也，言之必可行也。君子於其言，無所苟而已矣。

*Zilù said, "The ruler of Wei has been waiting for you, in order with you
to administer the government. What will you consider the first thing to
be done?"*

*The Master replied, "What is necessary is to rectify names." "So!
indeed!" said Zilù. "You are wide of the mark! Why must there be such
rectification?"*

*The Master said, "How uncultivated you are, Yu! A superior man,
regarding what he does not know, shows a cautious reserve.*

*"If names be not correct, language is not in accordance with the truth of
things. If language be not in accordance with the truth of things, affairs
cannot be carried on to success.*

*"When affairs cannot be carried on to success, proprieties and music do not
flourish. When proprieties and music do not flourish, punishments will not
be properly awarded. When punishments are not properly awarded, the
people do not know how to move hand or foot.*

*"Therefore, a superior man considers it necessary that the names he uses
may be spoken appropriately, and that what he speaks may be carried out
appropriately. What the superior man requires is just that in his words
there may be nothing incorrect."*

Not only Confucius, but also other Chinese and Western philosophers strongly condemned political correctness.
It is remarkable how fast our Western society adapted to political correctness. While in China, it is almost non-existent. Besides political correctness, our Western media is plagued by bias and prejudice, which is very damaging for the health of social relations. Newspeak, lack of sincerity and straightforward language in our media – has been around for much longer. Sometimes it is justified by the idea that the average person is unable to understand complex political processes.

Leo Tolstoy in *The Kingdom of God is Within You* said: "The most difficult subjects can be explained to the most slow-witted man if he has not formed any idea of them already; but the simplest thing cannot be made clear to the most intelligent man if he is firmly persuaded that he knows already, without a shadow of a doubt, what is laid before him."[10]

> It ain't what you don't know that gets you into trouble. It's what you know for sure that just ain't so.
>
> Mark Twain

In the long term, it will not only be our language but social cohesion in its entirety that will be affected. With destructive consequences for the economy and society. Political correctness is a slow but lethal killer.

---

10 Leo Tolstoy, "Царство Божіе внутри васъ, The Kingdom of God is Within You", *Berlin: August Deubner Verlag*, 1897, p.70.

Ignorance is the basis on which newspeak and bias can flourish. Hopefully the new internet media, and perhaps more travel and work in remote countries, will change that.

Mark Twain's famous saying still applies today:



Frank Sinatra in his song **My Way** says it like this:
For what is a man, what has he got?
If not himself, then he has naught
To say the things he truly feels
And not the words of one who kneels
The record shows I took the blows
And did it my way ...

China has no political correctness, straightforward language is part of daily life, it is ingrained in the Chinese language and in age-old traditions. It is a relief to be able to say and write what is on your heart.

Harbin M.I. Bookstore

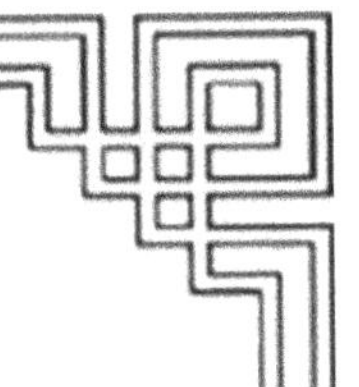



# 6.

# Propaganda.

*#propaganda #PR #public relations #culture #society #media*

In January 2003, some days before the start of the war in Iraq, there was a little Chinese girl on CCTV (China Central Television) who simply said: "There are no WMD's in Iraq" (Weapons of Mass Destruction). The little girl was running with open arms, a reference to Phan Thi Kim Phuc, the Vietnamese girl famously photographed running away for an American napalm attack.

The little girl on CCTV was China's answer to the American intelligence efforts to convince the world to start the war in Iraq. It was China's 'propaganda' answer to Colin Powell's U.N. Speech.[11]

The word 'propaganda' has a very negative connotation in almost all Western languages. It has the meaning of "information, especially of a biased or misleading nature, used to promote a political cause or point of view."[12]

Propaganda is usually attributed to regimes that have a different viewpoint to the Western ones. It is remarkable that Western media outlets use phrases such as *public relations* and *election campaign*, but when they refer to China, they use the word *propaganda*.

In China, the 中国工共产党央委员会宣传部 (Zhōngguó Gòngchǎndǎng Zhōngyāng Wěiyuánhuì Xuānchuánbù), the Chinese Communist Party Central Committee Propaganda Department is not seen as something negative at all. It is regarded

---

11 Jason Breslow: "Colin Powell's U.N. speech: A Great Intelligence Failure" in *Frontline* https://www.pbs.org/wgbh/frontline/article/colin-powell-u-n-speech-was-a-great-intelligence-failure/

12 "Propaganda: Definition of Propaganda by Lexico." *Lexico Dictionaries | English*, Lexico Dictionaries, www.lexico.com/en/definition/propaganda. https://www.lexico.com/en/definition/propaganda

as a *public relations* department of the CPC (Communist Party of China) in China.

**Propaganda** as per the old school definition **has 10 features**:

1. Keep it simple.
2. Repeat, repeat and repeat.
3. Be consistent.
4. Call up emotions.
5. Strengthen the group feeling.
6. Create an enemy.
7. Make your own truth.
8. Think authoritarian.
9. Transcend the here and now.
10. Focus on a broad audience.

Until some years ago, Chinese public relations efforts were almost exclusively focused on CPC members and the Chinese population. It is only recently that China is making slightly more of an effort to improve its image in Western media, but this does not yet go far enough. The worldwide Confucius Institutes (comparable with the German Goethe-Institute and the Académie française) are making valuable efforts to promote the Chinese culture in Europe and North America. Chinese embassies are buying advertisement space in newspapers and on social media. CCTV has branches in many capitals all over the globe.

It will be clear that most political or even scientific reports in the western media are meeting that definition more easily than whatever press release in the Chinese CPC 'mouthpiece' media.

In 1928 Edward Bernays published his seminal work, *Propaganda,* in which he argued that public relations is not a gimmick but a necessity. He wrote: "The conscious and intelligent manipulation of the organized habits and opinions of the masses is an important element in democratic society. Those who manipulate this unseen mechanism of society constitute an invisible government which is the true ruling power of our country. We are governed, our minds are moulded, our tastes formed and our ideas suggested, largely by men we have never heard of…. It is they who pull the wires that control the public mind."[13]



The Chinese public relation efforts are peanuts in comparison to the global influence of the American media, the Hollywood film industry and the global *lingua franca* status of the English language.

Chinese government propaganda is straightforward and unseasoned; the message is clear and unwrapped. Chinese people don't buy the 'sandwich-technique'. China is expressing its message like an engineer in a report to his manager.

China holds an extremely straightforward 'Do well and don't look back' attitude in its propaganda, both in China and abroad. **Therefore, because of its straightforwardness, Chinese propaganda is not half as efficient as Western propaganda.**

---

13   Edward L. Bernays, "Propaganda" New York, *Horace Liveright*, 1928
https://archive.org/details/BernaysPropaganda

## Propaganda posters

Jinan 1973
打倒美帝国主义！
Down with American imperialism !

*Fig. 9 Propaganda 1973*

Sanya 07.11.2018
The only 'propaganda' billboard I
have ever seen in China. It is quite
comparable with Western election
billboards.

*Fig. 10 Propaganda 2018*

In 1980, Deng Xiaoping abandoned the use of 'large character propaganda' along with the 'big four'[14] To justify that change, he used the constitution:

China's constitution clearly states that: "**citizens have the freedom to speak, communicate, publish, assemble, associate, march, demonstrate, and strike.**" These provisions guarantee the democratic rights that citizens should enjoy; while the "big four" are the opposite, hindering the legitimate democratic rights that citizens should receive.

China doesn't need internal propaganda; it does not have to spend

14   "The modification of the constitution, abandoning the big character propaganda" 21.03.2016
https://www.mala.cn/thread-13431588-1-1.html

resources on promoting national identity or social cohesion. It does not have to create a common enemy. It is the US that is setting up China as its enemy: President Trump with his daily tweets, the US deep state with sneaky attacks on China, the mainstream media with their half-truths. Foreign Ministry Spokespersons Geng Shuang and Hua Chunying only have to bring a simple, short reply during their regular press conference to inflate Chinese national cohesion. Repeated American attacks on China make China stronger as a nation. The global sales of Huawei boosted by 32% due to US restrictions on Huawei. The cost of the American 'marketing campaign' for Huawei was entirely paid with American tax money. The same is happening with China as a global brand name.

Beijing Tsinghua University Library

# 7.

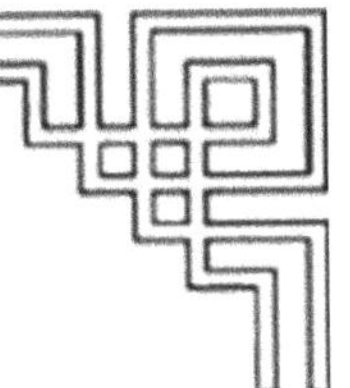

# The Big Sadness.

*#sadness #future #happiness #smile*

*China's success is that of its managing state, a state that has enabled the most populous country, in a quarter of a century, to set up an efficient digital infrastructure. The youngest half of the Chinese have lived through a continuous era of wealth growth and stability. There is a new level of adherence, particularly among young people, to the government's course.*

The chapter refers to the confidence the Chinese have in their respected government. The Chinese are content and have different reasons to be happy whereas the Europeans are typically distressed. A close Chinese friend visiting me in Europe asked me why European people look so serious or even sad all the time. I never noticed it, but indeed, he was right. Compared to China, we are grey people; we have an uncertain future. Our hope is fading away.

*Fig. 11 Lachklammern*

Driving through the streets of any Western city, typically filled with traffic congestion, one can easily notice the anger in the people's eyes in their cars. Either they're quarreling, shouting at the children in the rear seats or they do not communicate at all.

Then just walk through the streets of Chinese cities - watch the people, notice their smiles and joy. Why are they so much happier? Their smiles are ubiquitous and heart-warming. It is these little smiles that make Chinese society so different.

**Chinese people have many reasons to be happy.**
Their disposable income increases every year; their country and their economy is managed in an exemplary way. They have good reasons for their strong belief in a better future. From my extensive travels through the countryside villages in pre-opening, pre-economic-boom times, I remember those same honest, warm-hearted smiles; this makes me suspect that there must be causes other than purely material for the happiness of the Chinese people.

China is never boring. In China, one can see people of all kinds. They're strange, weird, funny, different… There's always something remarkable, something they do differently to Western people. There's never a dull day in China. Chinese people seem to love disordely chaos. They enjoy it.

China is crowded beyond imagination. When I first lived in Shanghai, I remember that I sometimes fled to a public park to avoid the crowds. Shortly afterwards, I got used to the bustle, but it was months before I could enjoy the loud ambiance of small local restaurants.

The only way to create welfare, prosperity for the people and social happiness is by a growing economy, a rising GDP. By <u>growing the cake</u>. Redistribution, cutting the cake in ever smaller pieces is counterproductive to poverty alleviation. China has found the right way to make its people happy.

Jiashan museum and Library

# 8.

# The Chinese Political System.

*#China #politics #subsidiarity #local #government #society*

The level of which a government connects with its people is very significant in the degree of which it is effective. Whether decision are made on central basis vs local authorities, often determines the advantages and disadvantages of an entire government. While centralised ideas create more unity, uniformity, and widespread legalities; local authorities often meet people's needs in more effective ways.

**China is a federal state:**

China is by no means a Jacobin state. In France, 'Jacobin' indicates a supporter of a centralized republican state with a strong central government. Jacobinism favours an extensive government intervention to transform society.

In China, however, the power of the central government is limited. Beijing serves as a guide. Financial and political power is in the hands of the provincial governors.

China sticks to the principles of subsidiarity: social and political issues should be dealt with at the most immediate local level, consistent with their resolution. At first sight it is a beautiful principle, but it is responsible for creating differences between provinces and cities in minimum wages, traffic fines, hùkǒu requirements, health care and more. The excessive power of the provinces sometimes causes friction with the central government.

In that way, China is **de facto a federal state**. But this is mentioned nowhere in the constitution.

**China is very different to what you think it is:**
Ray Dalio nailed it with his statement: "If you haven't spent time in China, you need to get any stereotypes you might have out of your mind because it's not how it was. This is not your father's communism. It is **Socialism with Chinese characteristics** that has been significantly and very effectively reformed, which has made it much more vital, creative, and economically free."[15]

**China, the election system:**
China has a reasonably fair system of local elections. Every three years, there are general elections in the whole nation for the People's Congresses. They rule over cities, city districts, counties, towns, townships and ethnic townships. All members of the People's Congresses are directly elected. There's no D'Hondt or Jefferson method to recalculate the votes to favour big parties or discourage small parties. A candidate only needs three supporters to get on the election list.

As per the Organic Law of Village Committees of the People's Republic of China each of the (more than one million) villages has to organize elections for the 'village chief', the mayor. Vote counting is as per the first-past-the-post ('the winner takes it all' system, similar to the UK, US and India.

At village level, there are usually very few Communist Party candidates-, sometimes none. In many villages the election battle is between the other, smaller parties.

---

15   Ray Dalio "Looking Back on the 40 Years of Reforms in China" *LinkedIn*, 03.01.2019. https://www.linkedin.com/pulse/looking-back-last-40-years-reforms-china-ray-dalio/

As per the Carter Center[16] that oversees China's elections, voter turnout is about 20% higher than America's.[17]

The specific issues and challenges associated with the Chinese elections are detailed in a paper by the Center for Democracy and Civil Society at Georgetown University *Electoral Administrative Framework for China*.[18]

## The 'three ups and three downs' system: [19]

1. The first 'up'
   The committee, responsible for the election's organisation, collects all the candidate nominations, verifies them, and publishes a first basic list.
2. The first 'down'
   The list is handed over to several groups of random citizens (voters) in every location for review.
3. The second 'up'
   The group representatives defend their review before the election committee, then makes an assessment to reduce the number of candidates.
4. The second 'down'

---

16   "The Carter Center on elections in China", *The Carter Center*, 20.10.2019
https://www.cartercenter.org/peace/china_elections/index.html
Liu Yawei, "China Elections and Governance", *Chinaelections*, 20.10.2019
http://www.chinaelections.org/
17   Godfree Roberts, "Democracy in China" *Quora*, 20.10.2019
https://www.quora.com/What-percentage-of-Chinese-people-want-democracy/answer/Godfree-Roberts
18   Prof. Jeff Fischer, Clara Barnett, Shuang Bin, Andrea Murta, Imara Crooms, David Jandura, SharonLazich, Bennett Seftel, Maegen Smith, Trishna Velamoor, and Christina Watts "Electoral Administrative Framework for China", *Georgetown University, Department of Government*, 01.12.2011.
http://aceproject.org/regions-en/countries-and-territories/CN/case-studies/local-elections-in-china
19   "China, election system" 20.10.2019
http://www.jzrd.gov.cn/zhuanti/gz/xxrdhjxj/xjzs/2006/0809/6540.html

The election group representatives' review reports are submitted to the voters for feedback.

5. The third 'up'

   The viewpoints of the voters are compiled and a report is made for the election committee. They decide on the final candidate list based on the feedback from the majority of the voters.

6. The third 'down'

   The final candidate list is published for the electorate.

It's quite complicated and time consuming, but it's very fair and just. Compare that with the compilation of candidate lists in most Western countries. In many European countries, the preparation of electoral candidate lists is accompanied by corruption, covert threats, extortion, media pressure, 'kaltstellung' (stripping authority), sometimes even 'political parricide'. And neither the voters, nor even the party members, have any input at all in the composition of the candidate lists. Western party politics and the party whip system have created a feudal dependence, away from Burke's 'general good, resulting from the general reason of the good' [20]

**Chinese politicians are engineers:**

In China, almost all politicians are STEM (Science Technology Engineering Mathematics) graduates. They apply *exact* science, sometimes called *hard* or *mathematical* science. They think and act in an engineering way. They're the exact opposite of sociologists. Faced with a problem, they analyse, compare, deduce, make a preliminary conclusion, test it out, verify and then decide. This may look complicated and time consuming, but they're doing this extremely quickly. Exactly like engineers.

In China, it's not just politicians but also human resource managers

---

20  Edmund Burke, *Speech to the Electors of Bristol.* 03.11.1774
http://press-pubs.uchicago.edu/founders/documents/v1ch13s7.html

and other 'sociology' professionals that are STEM graduates. In the West, which is rapidly moving away from STEM graduates to sociologists, the scientific method is regarded with distaste. But in China it works perfectly.

**The long-term vision:**Chinese politicians, in the same way as all Chinese people, have a long-term vision in mind. It's all about the future of their children and grandchildren.

In China, contrary to most Western countries, very little ad hoc law-making is required. Almost everything is analysed, discussed and prepared years in advance by think tanks, institutes and researchers at universities. Almost all law proposals are benchmarked with similar laws in other countries. New laws are usually tested out locally in two to five provinces, cities or districts.
Recently, Xi Jinping has encouraged all institutes and researchers to conduct even more polls, so as to have better contact with the real needs and concerns of the Chinese people.

The efficiency of the Chinese political system is breath-taking.

> Saying "Benchmark China" in the West is like swearing in the Chapel.
>
> Frans Vandenbosch

# The ruling rěn (rěn 忍):[21]

The Chinese are way too Confucian-Daoist-Buddhist to express their disillusionment to Westerners' faces outwardly, but among themselves, they can be quite open about it. From personal experience, I can say that a few rounds of beer or spirits can bring out the truth. I also hear it when speaking Mandarin with them. Once they realize that I really am on their side, they will vent their spleens, politely I might add. But again, most of the time, Westerners are clueless and kept in the dark.

All of this goes back to the ancient notion of rěn (忍) which means to forbear or endure. The top half of the Chinese character is a knife (刃) and the bottom half is the heart (心). as can be seen in the enlarged character below:

So, rěn is a knife coming down on top of you. You can't escape it and it is cutting into your heart. Not killing you, but hurting you, and you have to take it, endure it. The four parts which look like commas represent drops of blood. Rěn is serious business. Rěn is considered the apex of great leadership for Baba Beijing (China's leaders) and the ideal civilization among the citizens, between each other and other nations. There are dozens of different words and idioms centred on rěn and its concept of endurance, patience and tolerance.

---

21  Jeff J. Brown, "All the Chinese People Want is Respect" *Chinarising Puntopress*, 20.10.2019
http://chinarising.puntopress.com/2017/11/10/all-the-chinese-people-want-is-respect-aretha-franklin-diplomacy-on-china-rising-radio-sinoland-171110/

The Chinese endure endless foreign insults with a famous axiom, rěn bēi qiáng xiào (忍悲强笑), which means to endure sadness with a forced smile. Notice the second character for sadness (悲) also has the symbol for the heart at the bottom of the character.

In English, there is a similar saying: 'grin and bear it'. But Westerners do not base their entire system of governance and people's civilization on it. The Chinese do and have been doing so for 5000 years. Confucius codified it into statecraft and sociocultural protocol. Laozi made it into a philosophy (Daoism) and Buddha (albeit an Indian import) turned it into a world religion.

**Chinese politicians are smart:**
They are on average twenty-five IQ points smarter than Western politicians. To get to that bold conclusion, we first look at:

**1. Global IQ scores.** (as per Heiner Rindermann, Richard Lynn, Gerhard Meisenberg, Philippe Rushton & Arthur Jensen, Jason Richwine and the global SAT and PISA scores.)
Chinese people, in the developed coastal area and the less developed Western provinces, are *on average* 10 IQ points smarter than the *average* of the developed Western countries:

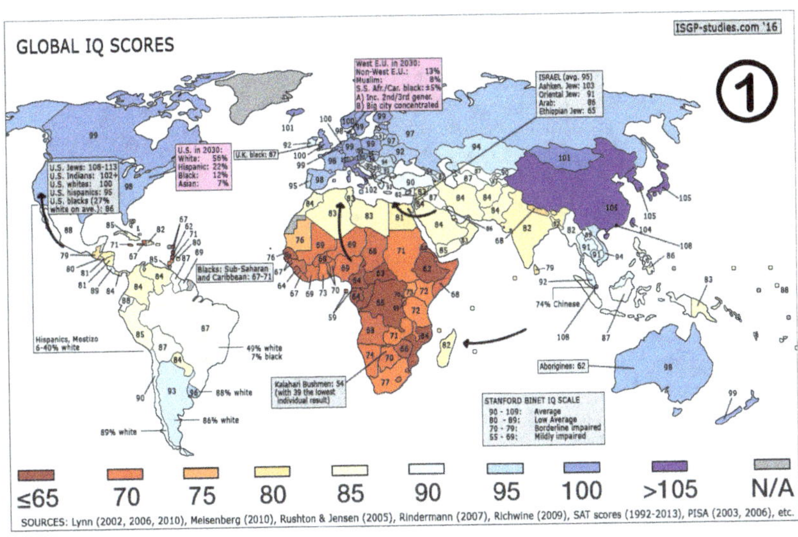


*Fig. 12 Global I.Q. Scores*

**2. Hard science versus soft science**. Hard science being science, technology, engineering and mathematics (STEM); soft 'science' being psychology, sociology, political science, law, communication, marketing, administration, education, history and anthropology.
In Western countries, almost all politicians are soft science graduates, while in China nearly all politicians are STEM graduates, most of them engineers.
Report by Dr Randal Olson, Lead Data Scientist at Life Epigenetics.[22] Based on data of the US National Center for

---

22   Randy Olson, "Average IQ of Students by College Major and Gender Ratio". *Randalolson*, 25.06.2014
http://www.randalolson.com/2014/06/25/average-iq-of-students-by-college-major-and-gender-ratio/

Education Statistics.[23]

Interactive scatter chart by Etienne Pinard.[24]

We can derive an average IQ difference of 15 points between STEM graduates and soft science graduates from this scatter chart.

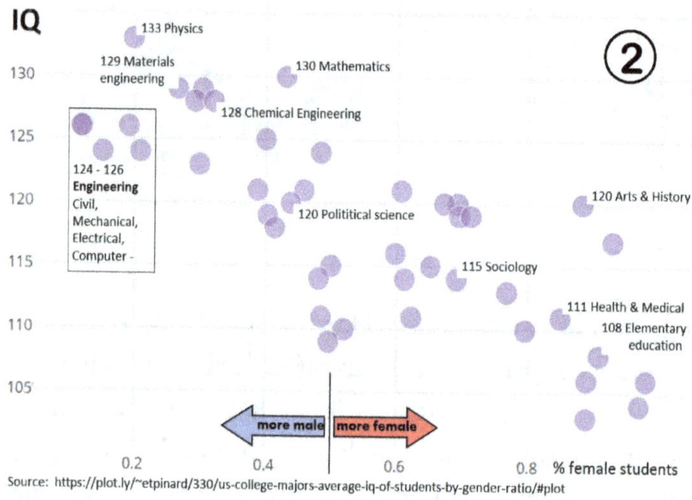


Fig. 13 IQ gap between STEM graduates and sociologists


23  Stephen Purcell, "Bachelor's, master's, and doctor's degrees conferred by postsecondary institutions, by sex of student and discipline division: 2018-19" NCES (US National Center for Education Statistics), 10.02.2021
https://nces.ed.gov/programs/digest/d19/tables/dt19_318.30.asp
24  Etienne Pinard, "Interactive Scatter Chart". *Plotly*, 07.10.2015.
https://plot.ly/~etpinard/330/us-college-majors-average-iq-of-students-by-gender-ratio/#/

When we add up ① and ② we get 10 + 15 = 25 points as shown in the graph here below:

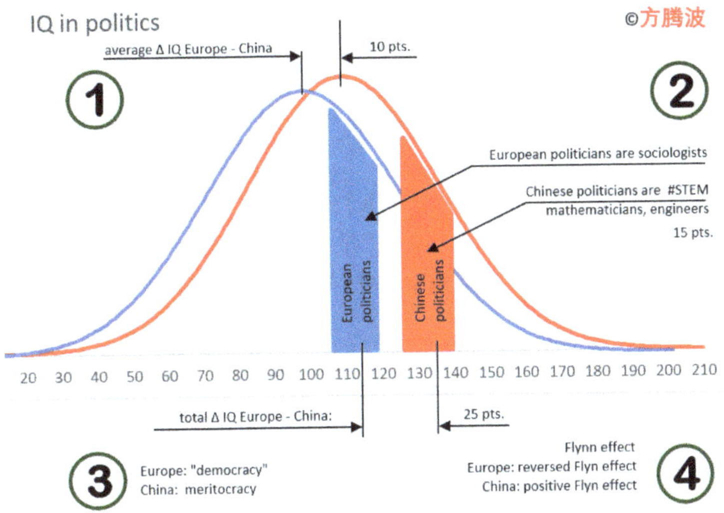


*Fig. 14 IQ in politics*

3. **Election versus meritocracy.** We don't even bring the IQ advantages of Europe's failing 'democracy' vs. China's efficient meritocracy into account. Godfree Roberts, in his article *Should we compete with China Can we?* [25] estimates that the Chinese meritocracy adds up the IQ of politicians to at least 140 points.

4. **The Flynn effect** (the global convention on how to adjust IQ scales over longer time periods) will certainly add up China's IQ scores. In Europe, due to mass immigration, there's currently a negative Flynn effect, while in China, due to the fast-developing education system, there's a positive Flynn effect.

---

25  Godfree Roberts, "Should We Compete with China? Can We?" *The UNZ Review,* 14.10.2019
http://www.unz.com/article/should-we-compete-with-china-can-we/

The West is becoming less intelligent. This is the shocking yet fascinating message of *'At Our Wits' End'*.[26]

**Obviously, these are averages** of averages. For sure there are smart politicians in Western countries too. But in China, due to the harsh, relentless meritocratic selection process, they're all smart – very smart.

Imagine a top-level negotiation of a large delegation of western versus Chinese politicians, sitting on opposite sides of the negotiation table. A 25 IQ points difference is easily noticeable!

26   Edward Dutton, Michael A. Woodley of Menie, Yr, "At Our Wits' End; Why We're Becoming Less Intelligent and What it Means for the Future" Societas collection at Imprint Academic, Exeter UK, 01.11.2018.
http://books.imprint.co.uk/book/?gcoi=71157100317440

Beijing CADG Innovation & Scientific
Research Demonstration Center

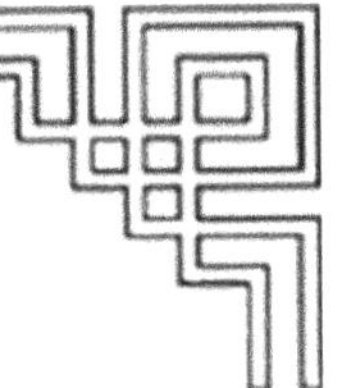

# Top-Level Politics.

*#politics #levels #standingcommittee #lawmaking #tianxia*

*As opposed to the western model of general overhead governing bodies, China has many different specific ministries, organisations and institutions. Such organs of society run with traditional values such as Tiānxià in mind. The variance and specific nature of each governing body allow for a more focused and detailed level of expertise.*

While a government is often seen as one major organisation; the way this large head is divided into subsets and sub-organs makes a substantial difference. China's way of specific ministries is important because this level of attention to detail is very rare to see anywhere else, particularly in the western world.

At both national and international level Chinese politics sticks to centuries old tiānxià principles.

Tiānxià (天下 all under heaven) should not be mixed up with 天命 tiānmìng, the mandate of heaven of the emperors.
Tiānxià is interwoven with traditional Chinese concepts such as 'nothing excluded' (wúwài 无外) and 'benevolent governance' (wángdào 王道) as a paradigmatic alternative to liberal cosmopolitanism or Eurocentric universalism.[27]

The Standing Committee of the Central Committee meets every Monday, Wednesday and Friday to take in the latest data and issue the latest directives to the government.

There's a voting system for the National Congress, but that's just a yes or no for (carefully) prepared law proposals.

---

27   Jun-Hyeok Kwak, "Global Justice without a Center: Reappraisal of Tiānxià with Non-domination." 20.10.2019
https://www.academia.edu/39343862/Global_Justice_without_a_Center_Reappraisal_of_Tianxia_with_Non-domination?email_work_card=view-paper

## National Institutions in China: [28]

National institutions are the general term for a set of state organs
established by the state to achieve its functions. According to
the provisions of Chapter III of the Constitution, China's state
institutions are composed of the National People's Congress, the
President of the People's Republic of China, the State Council,
the Central Military Commission, local people's congresses, local
people's governments at various levels and self-governing organs of
national autonomous areas. The state organs, the people's courts and
the people's procuratorates of the administrative region are composed.
From the perspective of the nature of exercising their powers, they
can be divided into power, administrative and judicial organs under
the principle of the unity of state power; from the geographical scope
of exercising their powers, they can be divided into central state
organs and local state organs. China has no Ministry of Internal
Affairs. The various services usually concentrated in the Ministry of
Internal Affairs in Western countries are in China dedicated to more
specialised ministries, institutions and departments.

China is, different from all other current countries, not a nation in
the Western sense but a Civilisation state.

China's politics is based on its long history and Confucianist
civilisation.[29] Therefore, China and the Chinese people can't be
conquerred. China, as a civilisation, has survived in the past and will
survive in the future whatever war or downfall.

---

28   Political and Political Theory Institute, "The National Institutions in China"
20.10.2019
http://www.baike.com/wiki/国家机构
29  Prof. Martin Jacques "When Will China Be the World's Most Powerful Country ?" in
an interview with Aaron Bastani on youTube. 09.04.2021.
https://www.youtube.com/watch?v=-3mP3Rb2g-I&t=2137s&ab_channel=MartinJacques

The complete list of the national institutions:

**National People's Congress (NPC)**
    Presidium
    Standing Committee
    General Office
    Secretariat
    Credentials Committee
    Motions Examination Committee
    Ethnic Affairs Committee
    Law Committee
    Finance and Economy Committee
    Foreign Affairs Committee
    Education, Science, Culture and Public Health Committee
    Committee for Internal and Judicial Affairs
    Overseas Chinese Affairs Committee
    Commission of Legislative Affairs
    Commission of Inquiry into Specific Questions
    Committee for Revision of the Constitution

**President of the People's Republic of China**

**Central Military Commission**

**Supreme People's Court**

**Supreme People's Procuratorate**

**State Council** (constitutionally synonymous with the Central People's Government)

    **Ministries and Commissions** Directly under the State Council

        Ministry of Foreign Affairs

        Ministry of National Defence

        State Development Planning Commission

        State Economic and Trade Commission

        Ministry of Education

        Ministry of Science and Technology

        Commission of Science, Technology and Industry for National Defence

        State Ethnic Affairs Commission

        Ministry of Public Security

        Ministry of State Security

        Ministry of Supervision

        Ministry of Civil Affairs

        Ministry of Justice

        Ministry of Finance

        Ministry of Personnel

        Ministry of Labour and Social Security

        Ministry of Land and Resources

        Ministry of Construction

        Ministry of Railways

        Ministry of Communications

        Ministry of Information Industry

        Ministry of Water Resources

        Ministry of Agriculture

        Ministry of Foreign Trade and Economic Cooperation

        Ministry of Culture

        Ministry of Public Health

        State Family Planning Commission

People's Bank of China
State Auditing Administration

**Offices** under the State Council
General Office of the State Council
Office of Overseas Chinese Affairs
Hong Kong and Macao Affairs Office
Taiwan Affairs Office
Office of Legislative Affairs
Office for Economic Restructuring
Research Office of the State Council
Information Office

**Departments** Directly under the State Council
General Administration of Customs
State Taxation Administration
State Environmental Protection Administration
Civil Aviation Administration of China (CAAC)
State Administration of Radio, Film and Television
State Sport General Administration
State Statistics Bureau
State Administration of Industry and
Commerce (MOFCOM)
Press and Publication Administration
State Copyright Bureau
State Forestry Bureau
State Bureau of Quality and Technical Supervision
State Drug Administration (SDA)
State Intellectual Property Office (SIPO)
National Tourism Administration
State Bureau of Religious Affairs
Counsellors' Office of the State Council

Government Offices Administration of the State Council

**Institutions** Directly under the State Council
  Xinhua News Agency
  Chinese Academy of Sciences
  Chinese Academy of Social Sciences
  Chinese Academy of Engineering
  Development Research Centre of the State Council
  National School of Administration
  China Earthquake Administration
  China Meteorological Administration

A simplified overview:

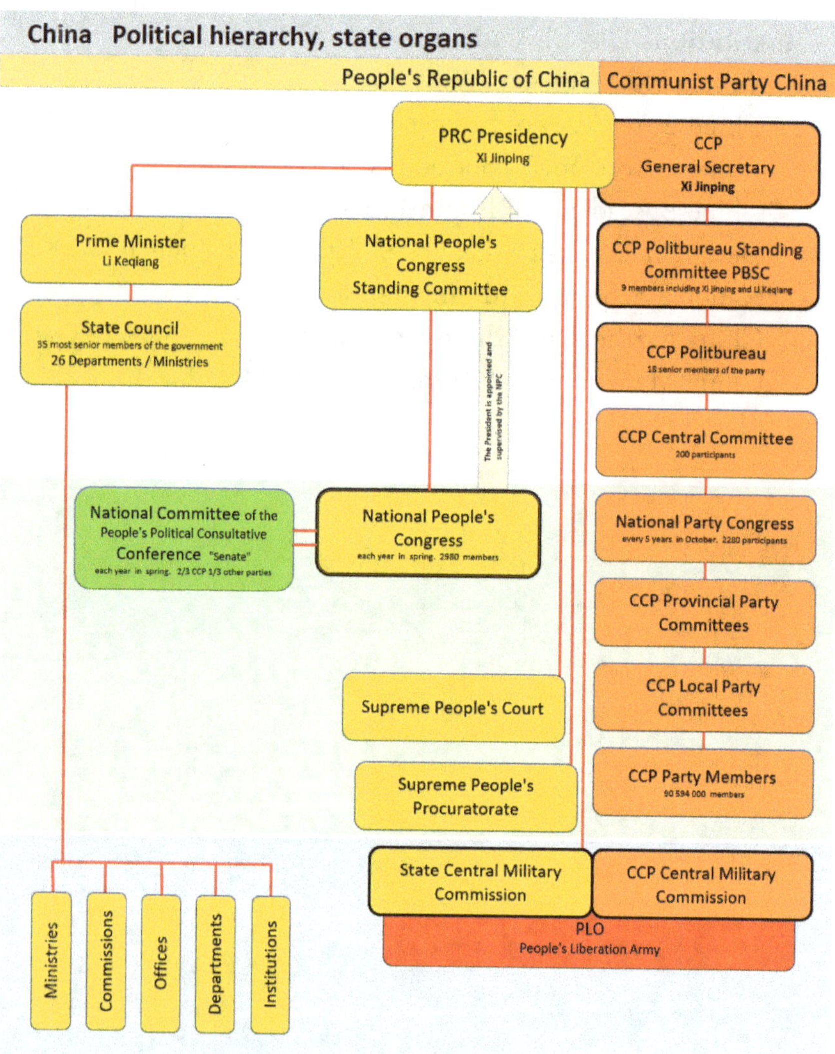


Fig. 15 China, political hierarchy and state organs

Shenzhen Resources Archives Library

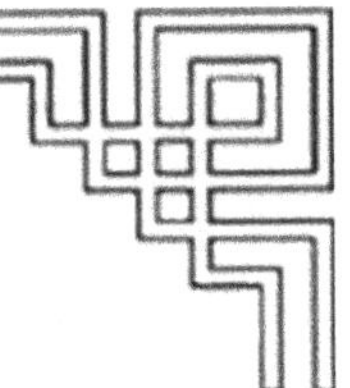

Chapter

# 10.

# The Chinese Economy.

*#economy #Shimomuran #Wernerian #macroeconomic #SOE #western–viewpoints*

*The western media has always been misinformed about not only the structure of China's economics but also the success that it achieves. The Shimomuran–Wernerian Macroeconomics style of economic policy has led to China collecting the positive features of capitalism and socialism. Economic growth factors such as the stock market and production are on the rise, such as a capitalistic country, 90% of families own a house like the ideals of a fair, equal communist regime.*

Economy is the setting stone for much of the scenery that exists in a country. Many sociologists would say that class differences are what initiate other differences and traits in a population. It is important to discuss China's economic systems because of the success that this country has had. Further-more, educating ourselves and others about how the Chinese economy is misrepresented is a must.

Economy is stronger than politics. Politicians in any political system can only resist or deny economic developments for so long. But in the long term, they have to bend and adapt to the reality.

## Shimomuran-Wernerian Macroeconomics

Long before China's economic wonder, there was Wang Anshi (1021–1086) a Chinese Transcendental who was the Finance Minister (1070/76) and confidant of Shenzong, Emperor during the Song dynasty.[30]

The sheer breadth of his capabilities - his "New [Economic] policies" involving greater credit creation, his continual actions to improve the lot of the majority of the people, his actions in favour of democracy, his outstanding poetry and essays, and his continual

---

30  George Tait Edwards, UK entrepreneur, thinker and experienced manager, author of a number of books. "How did Wang Anshi contribute to the economic world?" 19.10.2018 https://www.quora.com/How-did-Wang-Anshi-contribute-to-the-economic-world

position as an innovator opposed by the conservatives - qualify him as a Transcendental, a multitalented person with a notable and direct effect on the history of China and thus by his example upon the history of the human race.

Wang Anshi's economic contributions were immense - he broke up monopolies, and acted to establish future firms to provide their products and services, ensured the greater creation of credit (which is one of the "secrets" of currently rapid Chinese economic growth) improved the amazing Chinese meritocratic selection system for Civil Servants by adding math to their exams, made the National Academy into a genuine academic forerunner of many of today's Universities, and provided pensions for the old and unemployed in the first historical stirrings of the welfare state. Under his rule, the state also began to institute public orphanages, hospitals, dispensaries, hospices, cemeteries, and reserve granaries.

Today, the Chinese economy is not at all Keynesian. In the last four decades, the economy has gradually become Shimomuran - Wernerian.[31] Shimomuran(-Wernerian) Macroeconomics was first 'invented' and applied by a Japanese team in Manchuria during the 1920s.[32] It fell into oblivion during Mao Zedong but and was full scale re-established by Deng Xiaoping. It is sometimes called 'Investment Credit Economics'. It is based on a 'sound fiscal policy', that is, a balanced government budget. The application in China of Shimomuran-Wernerian Macroeconomic policy has resulted in explosive, unprecedented growth of economy and prosperity. An economic miracle, never previously seen in other times or places.

---

31   Richard A. Werner, "Princes of the Yen - Japan's Central Bankers and the Transformation of the Economy", Quantum Publishers, ISBN-13: 978-0765610492; 01.02.2003 https://quantumpublishers.com/quantum_publishers_book_shop.html
32   George Tait Edwards, "What is Shimomuran Economics", *Quora*, 07.03.2017 https://www.quora.com/What-is-Shimomuran-economics

Shimomuran-Wernerian Macroeconomics has been applied in China from the mid-1970s to the present day - with economically miraculous results.

Most western media outlets refuse to understand this phenomenon or investigate China's economic boom's underlying triggers. Instead, they simply deny the economic developments, or, worse, predict the rapid collapse of the economy in China:

**Historical economic predictions about China:[33]**

Three decades of lies about the Chinese economy:

1990. The Economist: 'China's economy has come to a halt.'
1996. The Economist: 'China's economy will face a *hard landing*.
1998. The Economist: 'China's economy entering a dangerous period of *sluggish growth*.'
1999. Bank of Canada: 'Likelihood of a *hard landing* for the Chinese economy.'
2000. Chicago Tribune: 'China currency move nails *hard landing* risk coffin.'
2001. Wilbanks, Smith& Thomas: 'A *hard landing* in China.'
2002. West Chester University: 'China Anxiously Seeks a *Soft Economic Landing*.'
2003. The New York Times: 'Banking crisis imperils China.'
2004. The Economist: 'The *great fall* of China?'
2005. Nouriel Roubini: 'The Risk of a *Hard Landing* in China.'
2006. The International Economy: 'Can China Achieve a *Soft Landing*?'
2007. TIME: 'Is China's Economy Overheating? Can China avoid a

---

33  Mazhouma in a comment to Alec Fahrin, "The World Economy is Picking Up", *the Economist* 21.03.2017.
https://www.economist.com/node/21718866/comments?sort=2

*hard landing?'*
2008. Forbes: '*Hard Landing* in China?'
2009. Fortune: 'China's *hard landing*. China must find a way to recover.'
2010. Nouriel Roubini: '*Hard landing* coming in China.'
2011. Business Insider: 'A Chinese *Hard Landing* May Be Closer Than You Think.'
2012. The American Interest: 'Dismal Economic News from China: A *Hard Landing*.'
2013. Zero Hedge: 'A *Hard Landing* in China.'
2014. CNBC: 'A *hard landing* in China.'
2015. Forbes: 'You Got Yourself a Chinese *Hard Landing*.'
2016. The Economist: '*Hard landing* looms for China.'
2017. The National Interest: 'Is China's Economy *Going to Crash*?'
2018. McKinsey: 'China faces a choice: Modernise or risk a *very hard landing*'
2019. Forbes: 'The China *Hard Landing* Is Back on The Table'

The pattern is quite clear, isn't it? The *'Hard Landing'* they were hoping for, never came.


**How people in China afford their outrageously expensive homes[34]**
The people of China can afford to buy extremely expensive properties. In fact, 90% of families in the country own their home, giving China one of the world's highest home ownership rates. What's more is that 80% of these homes are owned outright, without mortgages or other loans. On top of this, according to Nomura International, more than 20% of urban households own more than one home.

---

34  Wade Shephard, "How People in China Afford Their Outrageously Expensive Homes", *Forbes*, 30.03.2016
https://www.forbes.com/sites/wadeshepard/2016/03/30/how-people-in-china-afford-their-outrageously-expensive-homes/#1f244bf4a3ce

## Is the Chinese economy communist, socialist or capitalist?[35]

In practice the Chinese economy has several different features which makes it difficult to classify. On the one hand, the Chinese economy has characteristics that would disqualify it from being a liberal market economy:

China has seriously reduced, but still has a lot of SOE's (State-Owned Enterprises) which coexist alongside a large private sector; however, the exact size of the state sector is difficult to calculate because many nominally private publicly listed firms are partially owned by central, provincial and municipal state entities.

China directs its economy through a state-owned financial system to meet industrial policy and plan objectives through various incentives. This state-directed activity extends to SEI's (Strategic Emerging Industries), private enterprises that the central government has targeted for growth.

Politically and ideologically the Communist Party of China is committed to the long-term development of socialism. It describes its current economic system as a 'Socialist market economy with Chinese Characteristics'.

There have been proposals in Shenzhen to establish a social dividend, financed from the return on state-owned enterprises, but this is more prospective since China is not sufficiently developed yet for any comprehensive social dividend scheme. Nevertheless, a key characteristic of socialism is eliminating the system of wage labour

---

35  Sean Ahluwalia, "Is China's economy closest to market socialism, free market capitalism, or state capitalism?", *Quora*, 22.06.2019
https://www.quora.com/Is-Chinas-economy-closest-to-market-socialism-free-market-capitalism-or-state-capitalism

and the distinction between owners and workers. A social dividend system erodes away at this distinction and gives meaning to 'social ownership of the means of production'.

**On the other hand, the Chinese economy has the foundational elements of a capitalist economy:**

1.  **Different from most European SOE's**, China's State-Owned Enterprises are organized as corporate entities and *primarily operate to maximize profits*. They are not integrated into a single entity or network. In that way, Chinese SOE's are more 'capitalist', more free market, than most of the European SOE's.
2.  **The existence of stock exchanges** and private ownership through a stock market is a central feature of capitalism. Most listed state-owned enterprises are under 'mixed ownership' where private entities can own minority shares in SOEs.
3.  **The wage-labour relationship** is in full effect (see my above point on the social dividend) and capitalists and financial speculators exist. By extension, classes exist based on the ownership of capital.
4.  **The accumulation of capital** is in full play and exists within the framework of a global market capitalist system, and thus operates under the law of value. In this sense, it does not represent a fundamentally different form of economic system from other capitalist economies at the systemic level.

**The Chinese economy is immune to a Western-style financial crisis** caused by debt because China's financial system is state-owned and integrated with debt incurred by state-owned institutions. China's debt is mainly used to finance investment rather than consumption. The Shimomuran-Wernerian Macroeconomics in full play. Also, due to the integrated nature of the financial system, the state can simply write off bad debt to avoid a 'hard landing' *in exactly the same way as big Western MNC's.*

*We can conclude that China's current economic system is somewhere between a directed market capitalism, similar to France, and market socialism, but is still functionally capitalist.*

**Marx would not like it.**

Hefei Central Smart Garden Library

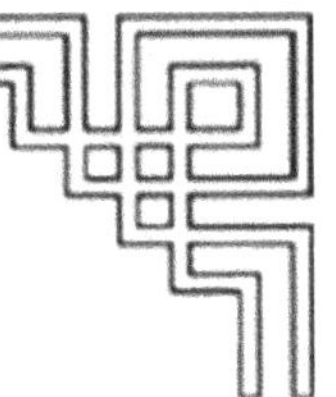



# 11.

# True Communism, Mao Zedong-style.

*#communism #socialism #Mao Zedong*
*#Dazhai #Nanjie #Huaxi*

*The red star still decorates the flag of the People's Republic of China but is the country still communist? The Chinese system is both pragmatic and ideological. It tolerates an important private sector, but under the watchful control of the planning state.*

The chapter underlines the true roots of communism still practised in some parts of China. These days, it is near impossible to find convinced communists in China. In some rare places, there are remnants of the Mao era, an attempt to keep the old style communism alive:

There are at least three, maybe five villages in China where they make efforts to live and work in the true communist way. Some rural villages claim to be the last bastions of the country's socialist past. But not all residents are as happy or as equal as they'd like to be.

**China's Collective Villages Struggle to Keep It Together** [36]

Henan, Central China — The sun rises on a chill November morning in Nanjie, illuminating a giant statue of Mao Zedong in the village's central square. Behind the former Chinese leader, a giant wall-poster honours four other towering figures of communism: Karl Marx, Friedrich Engels, Vladimir Lenin, and Josef Stalin.

Mao casts a long shadow over Nanjie in more ways than one. On the surface, the government of the 3000-strong village has retained a collectivist social system reminiscent of the Mao era, guaranteeing residents full employment, free housing, free health care, and subsidized college education.

In doing so, Nanjie offers a rebuttal to the conventional wisdom of China's four decades of economic reform. The policy — officially

---

36   Fu Danni and Wang Yiwei, "China's collective villages" *Sixth Tone*, 20.12.2018. http://www.sixthtone.com/news/1003362/chinas-collective-villages-struggle-to-keep-it-together

known as 'reform and opening-up' — has largely seen the state move away from rigid central planning and political dogma, instead allowing the market economy to take over. In doing so, China has transformed from an economic backwater into the world's largest economy, lifting hundreds of millions out of poverty in the process.

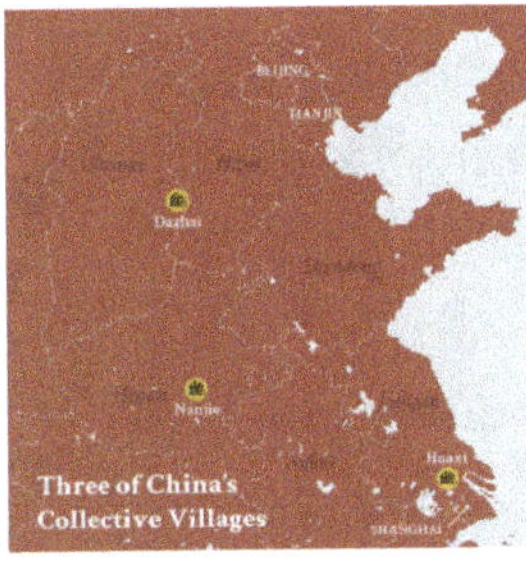


Dazhai, Shanxi province
Nanjie, Henan province
Huaxi, Jiangsu provincee

*Fig. 16 Dazhai, Shanxi province; Nanjie, Henan province Huaxi, Jiangsu province*

But Nanjie, along with other pockets of China, have partly retained the former political model. They are the country's so-called collective villages — small, often isolated settlements that retain the pre-reform socialist system's vestiges. Many such villages are openly nostalgic for a time when Mao was China's paramount leader and the state, at least on paper, looked after its citizens from cradle to grave.

In practice, collective villages are less like throwbacks to the Mao era, and more like businesses: The village government owns and operates a corporation, residents work for it, and the corporation, in turn, plows its profits back into salaries, perks, and village infrastructure. By and large, this system leaves residents feeling wealthy and well looked-after.

But when utopian social ideology collides with aggressive business models, conflict is inevitable. In Nanjie, for instance, individualistic young people struggle to connect emotionally with the collective's spirit of self-sacrifice. On the other hand, in eastern China's Jiangsu province, Huaxi claims to be the 'richest village in China', but some residents complain its economic success has created a privileged class of villagers who lord it over their neighbours. And in Dazhai, a village once lauded by Mao himself as a shining beacon of socialism, long-term economic malaise has pushed residents into tourism tinged with Maoist nostalgia — with mixed results.

What can collective villages' experiences tell us about how China balances ideology, economy, and the desire to preserve social order? Over the course of several months, Sixth Tone's reporters visited Nanjie, Huaxi, and Dazhai to find out.

**Utopia, Redefined**

Nanjie officials position the village as a kind of modern-day socialist utopia, hamming up its so-called Red culture - a celebration of the history of communism in China and Party rule. Older villagers in particular laud a deep sense of camaraderie and welcome protection from the more cutthroat aspects of the market economy. "There are no worries around here, no pressure," says 56-year-old Cui Miaoyun, a long-time resident of Nanjie who works at the local noodle factory. "The village takes care of us: from education, to marriage, and finally, to death."

**There are no worries around here, no pressure ... The village takes care of us. - Cui Miaoyun, Nanjie resident**

But in reality, Nanjie's capitalist business model is hard to ignore. The local government runs Nanjie Village Group, a conglomerate that produces everything from plastic packaging to instant noodles and corporate printing services. The government guarantees villagers a job at the group, paying them 30 % of their salary in cash and putting the remaining 70 % into public services like housing, health care, and university grants. Authorities also keep tabs on its citizens' behaviour via a complex 10-point ranking system. Nanjie's government even holds communal wedding ceremonies and provides free cremation and burial services.

Although not as wealthy as more developed parts of rural China, the living standards in Nanjie are higher than in other Henan villages. The government's redistribution policy means that there is relatively little difference between rich and poor. But life in Nanjie isn't as harmonious as it seems. Instead of income inequality, the village is struggling to bridge the gap between community-minded older residents and increasingly individualistic younger generations.

**When I hear old Communist songs playing over the roadside loudspeakers, I feel very nostalgic. - An, tourist**

Western communism is in no way comparable with Huaxi, Nanjie, Dazai or the communism in the pre Deng Xiaoping era. Western communists, in the US as well as in Europe are way more fanatical.

**Communism in the US:**
In the US, as per a recent Rasmussen Reports national telephone survey, 11% of likely U.S. voters think communism is morally superior to the American system of politics and economics.[37]

---

37  "Communism, National Survey of 1000 Likely Voters", *Rasmussen Reports*, 12.03.2011 http://www.rasmussenreports.com/public_content/politics/questions/pt_survey_questions/march_2011/questions_communism_march_12_13_2011

Nanning Garden Art Museum

# 12.

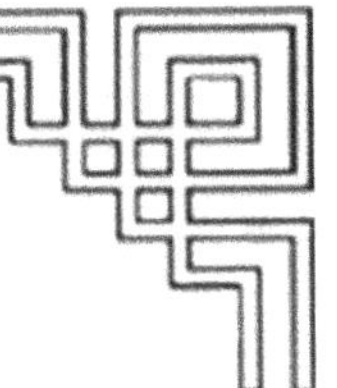

# A Tale of Two Systems.

*#communism #democracy #socialism #capitalism #meritocracy*

*Elections are a part of, but not equal to democracy. Perhaps the most significant part of democracy is financial freedom and stability. Many western countries rely on strict partisan policies which find it hard to adapt and evolve. China, on the other hand, understands that the most progressive and growth forward way of operating is by mixing different schools of thought into perfection.*

Democracy is arguably the most commonly used term in the west to separate themselves from others in the public eye. However, it is important to question the legitimacy of said democracy and how effective it truly is in democracy. Whilst democracy sounds good to the ear, on the large scale; it has many issues that China has fixed by altering some processes.

In our Western thinking, it is a standard assumption that it eventually becomes a capitalist, multi-party democracy as a society progresses.

**Eric X. Li, a Chinese investor and political scientist, begs to differ.** In his provocative, boundary-pushing talk, 'A Tale of Two Political Systems'[38], he asks his audience to consider that there's more than one way to run a successful modern nation. What he found punches holes in our assumptions about China's limitations. Too many people think that the one-party system must be operationally rigid, politically closed, morally illegitimate. In fact, he argues, the opposite is true: what defines China's one-party system is adaptability, meritocracy and legitimacy.[39]

---

38  Eric X. Li, "A Tale of two Political Systems", *TED Talks on YouTube*, 01.07.2013
https://www.youtube.com/watch?v=s0YjL9rZyR0
39  Karen Frances Eng about Eric X. Li, "A Tale of Two Systems" *TED Blog Global*, 13.06.2013
https://blog.ted.com/a-tale-of-two-systems-eric-x-li-at-tedglobal-2013/

It looks like Winston Churchill's saying "It has been said that democracy is the worst form of government, except all those others that have been tried"[40], is no longer valid. The Chinese capitalist meritocracy seems to work exceptionally well. There's no other country or political system on this globe that has lifted more than a billion people out of poverty so fast and that can boast such high ratings of 'customer satisfaction'.

Jill Stein said it in a much more straightforward way: "Democracy is not what we don't want. Democracy is what we do want. It is a set of affirmative values by which we can move forward. If we cannot insert our values into our vote, and our vote is simply against what we fear most, then we are a ship lost at sea ..."[41]

Yasheng Huang, MIT (Massachusetts Institute of Technology) researcher, wrote in his book *Capitalism with Chinese Characteristics; Entrepreneurship and the State* that "The economic theory in China is not socialism with Chinese characteristics, but the opposite: capitalism with Chinese characteristics"[42] As explained in detail in Chapter 11.

**Don't mix up elections with democracy:**
Don't be fooled into thinking that the only road to reform is through the ballot box. Whether you vote or don't vote doesn't really matter. What matters is what else you're doing to push back against government incompetence, abuse, corruption, graft, fraud

---

40   "Parliament bill" *HC Deb vol 444 cc203-321*, 11.11.1947.
https://api.parliament.uk/historic-hansard/commons/1947/nov/11/parliament-bill#column_206
41   Jill Stein "Jill Stein Quotes about Democracy", *BrainyQuote.com*, 20.10.2019.
https://www.brainyquote.com/quotes/jill_stein_764067
42   Yasheng Huang, "Capitalism with Chinese Characteristics; Entrepreneurship and the State", *Cambridge.org*, ISBN 9780521898102, 01.09.2008
https://www.cambridge.org/us/academic/subjects/economics/public-economics-and-public-policy/capitalism-chinese-characteristics-entrepreneurship-and-state?format=HB

and cronyism. After all, argues John W. Whitehead, there is more to citizenship than the act of voting for someone who, once elected, will march in lockstep with the of the powers-that-be.[43]

**Empires and nations**; their power, language, industrial development, degree of democracy, …

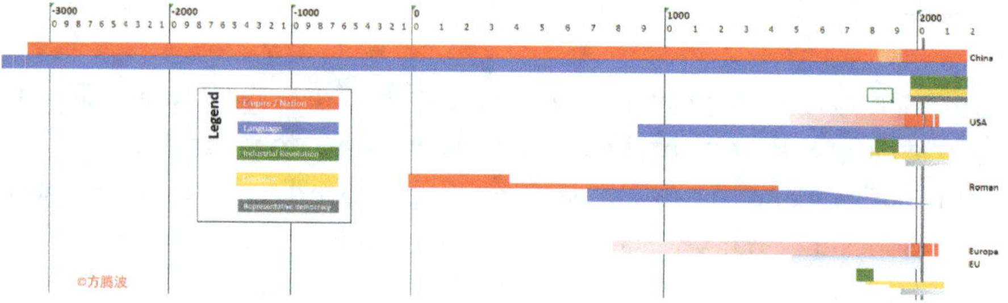


Fig. 17 Empires and nations

# The rise and fall of empires as per Ray Dalio in The Changing World Order: The Big Cycles Over the Last 500 Years[44]

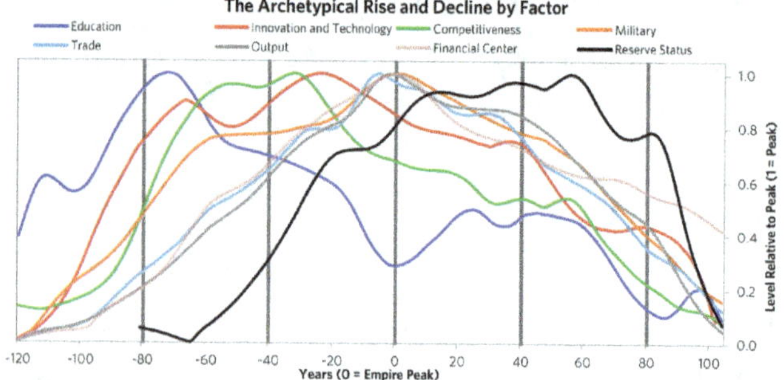


Fig. 17a  Rough estimates of relative standing of great empires.

---

43   John W. Whitehead, "If Voting Made Any Difference, They Wouldn't Let Us Do It" *The Rutherford Institute*, 01.08.2016
https://rutherford.org/publications_resources/john_whiteheads_commentary/if_voting_made_any_difference_they_wouldnt_let_us_do_it
44   Ray Dalio, "The Changing World Order: The Big Cycles Over the Last 500 Years" GuruFocus.com 22.05.2020
https://finance.yahoo.com/news/ray-dalio-commentary-changing-world-202256827.html?.

Haikou The Wormhole Library

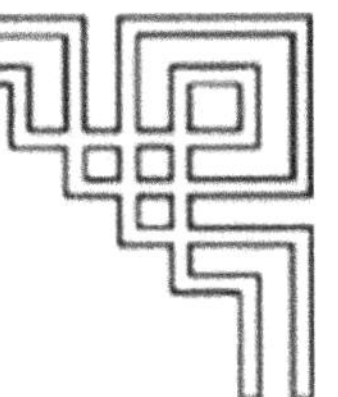

# About Democracy, the Real One.

*#democracy #elections*

*Democracy is a vulnerable system with various flaws and holes. Despite the western depiction of democracy, it is clear that the results of so-called "democracy" fail all the time. Whether it is the limitation of long-term planning or the popularity battle created between candidates, democracy certainly fails to adequately guarantee a better future. China's government not only gets pressured by the people to do better, but the long term and short-term goals are deeply engaged with the democracy and freedom of individuals.*

One of the failures of western democracy is how it creates almost a bid-ding war or popularity contest in every facet of life. This type of democracy can prevent continuity and homogeny. It must be considered whether democracy is pretty in image only or whether it is truly the ideal way of governance.

**About the definition and limits of democracy**

The western widespread idea that elections are democracy is lunatic. They are not because:

- Elections can only choose between very limited pre-selected choices. The Pre-selections aren't even linked to what people might want.
- Few, if any, counting systems that give everyone a vote of the same value.
- Most political decisions are complex and nuanced. None of these can be considered in an election. Only a cartoon version where people are chosen instead of people choosing.

民主 (mínzhǔ) is the Chinese translation of democracy, literally means "people make the decision" (not necessarily through elections.)

Most of the English language dictionaries mention "elections" in the definition of democracy. That's a tricky inaccuracy.

Merriam Webster is a bit more careful. They define democracy as:

1. a government by the people especially rule of the majority
2. a government in which the supreme power is vested in the people and exercised by them directly or indirectly through a system of representation usually involving periodically held free elections

The Larousse definition of democracy:
1. Système politique, forme de gouvernement dans lequel la souveraineté émane du peuple.
2. État ayant ce type de gouvernement.

They come close.

Albert Einstein (Ulm 1879-Princeton 1955) unconsciously spoke out for the kind of democracy as today in China:

> "Mein politisches Ideal ist das demokratische. Jeder soll als Person respektiert und keiner vergöttert sein."
>
> Albert Einstein

Democracy does not make countries stronger. It comes with severe liability that only countries that are already sufficiently developed can withstand and stay developed. The underlying mechanism can be easily formulated as well:

On any particular problem that requires specific expertise, most people will lack expertise, make wrong decisions, and inevitably empower such decisions through mass voting.

On any particular problem that requires long-term planning and temporary trade-offs, most people will vote against the trade-offs, so that the long-term planning cannot proceed under the democratic system of regular votes to choose the next administration.

In any system that chooses the next administration through popular voting, candidates will be more inclined to focus on winning votes than solving actual problems, especially when the problems require long-term planning and temporary trade-offs.

Therefore, western 'democracies' are bound to be incapable of solving problems. They are only successful because such problems have been solved or are willing to be solved using non-democratic means.

On the other hand, non-democracies, while susceptible to the whims of a smaller group of ruling class, at least have a chance of the rulers making the correct choice.

Of course, this is not saying non-democracies should be expected to be stronger instead. Only that the current success of democracies depends on many factors unrelated to democracy, and democracies should not be expected to be generally stronger than non-democracies.

## Elites, Interest Groups and Average Citizens in Politics[45]
## in western politics

Despite the sometimes-chaotic election results, and despite many
criticisms of the median-voter theorem as simplistic and empirically
inapplicable or wrong, a good many scholar still clings to the
idea that the policy preferences of the median voter tend to drive
policy outputs from the western political system. A fair amount of
empirical evidence has been adduced.

**The fly in the ointment is that none of this evidence allows for, or
explicitly assesses, the impact of such variables as the preferences
of wealthy individuals**, or the preferences and actions of organized
interest groups, which may independently influence public policy
while perhaps being positively associated with public opinion, thereby
producing a spurious statistical relationship between opinion and policy.

A major challenge to majoritarian pluralist theories is posed by the
argument that collective action by large, dispersed sets of individuals
with individually small but collectively large interests tends to be
prevented by the 'free rider' problem. Barring special circumstances
(selective incentives, by-products, coercion), individuals who would
benefit from collective action may have no incentive to form or
join an organized group personally. If everyone thinks this way and
lets George do it, the job is not likely to get done. This reasoning
suggests that 'potential groups' may be unlikely to form, even if
millions of peoples' interests are neglected or harmed by government.
Aware of the collective action problem, officials may feel free to

---

45  Martin Gilens and Benjamin I. Page, "Testing Theories of American Politics: Elites,
Interest Groups, and Average Citizens" *Cambridge.org*, 18.09.2014
https://www.cambridge.org/core/journals/perspectives-on-politics/article/testing-theories-
of-american-politics-elites-interest-groups-and-average-citizens/62327F513959D0A304D
4893B382B992B/core-reader

ignore much of the population and act against the average citizen's interests.


# Democracy in China




**China has real democracy.**[46]

After living in China for some decades, I learned that most Chinese people don't care at all whether China is a called a democracy or not. They care very much whether or not the party is implementing government in a fair way to *most* people and promotes the building of wealth for its citizens. Many Chinese people **speak out when controversial events happen that suggests the party is not adequately acting in the citizens'** interest.

Ladies and gentlemen, *if this is not what a real democracy should be like, I don't know what is.*

**Demos = people** and **kratein = to rule**

Rule by people means either direct democracy, which is not adopted by any modern state of a considerable size, maybe except Switzerland to a certain degree. There's no direct democracy in the US, not the UK, not in Germany, or, more realistically, a state that cares about

---

46   Brian Sloan, reposted by Mei Hualong (Harvard Uni) "Don't people in China want to live in a democracy?" *Quora reposted on Narkive,* 18.12.2018. https://soc.culture.china.narkive.com/qP821quB/don-t-people-in-china-wish-to-live-in-a-democratic-country-so-the-answer-is-yes-we-do-hope-that-we

most of its citizens' long-term benefits. Election and "representative democracy" does not mean democracy; China has elections on different levels, though this is another issue.

To be the ruler can also mean that you are the lord.

And someone who is forced to cast a ballot to choose between two partisan candidates that care more about themselves and the elites they represent, pretending that he can influence the fate of his country, is not a lord, but a slave – or better, a tool, an instrument, a dehumanized object to decorate a system that serves the elites and calls itself "democracy".

In China, if you don't care about politics, it's up to you, there are other things that can attract your interest. The government will provide you with basic care if you are in dire needs, but you need to work hard to improve your living standards most of the time.

If you care about politics and have spent some time reading news, history, political science, economics and the like, you will gradually be glad that the state is still run by a group of people who know what they are doing. People like Mr. Xi Jinping and others make plans whose results and outcomes they will never possibly see in their lifetime. It is good to have civil servants and leaders who hold themselves against the standards of scientists and researchers who care about the future, rather than the current or the next term. If you want to exert more influence, be a civil servant and climb up the ladder to become influential; or at least work in media or think tanks or research institutions; or become a relatively successful businessperson.

As an average citizen caring about your community and you're

dissatisfied, there are many things you can do in China: you can get
easily in touch with different branches of the local government that
are in charge of different affairs, get in touch with the local village
council or resident council, get in touch with the representative
of the local people's congress, report to media or government
departments on Weibo.

I used to write to our municipal and district governments on an
online platform to report and complain about many things, bad road
quality, etc. And I got a polite and informative response each and
every time. Not all problems can be solved all at once, but I did feel
respected, and some problems were indeed resolved quite fast.

China is trying to upgrade its industry and is focusing on top
technologies. For us, westerners, the market is a tool, not a god. But
in China, there are plans to encourage each field while utilizing
market economy to promote competition between leading Chinese
brands and manufacturers. Although many of the policies and their
implementation are not necessarily perfect, an average citizen like
myself feels lucky that we can see where the path leads to.

And meanwhile our western media debate about whether Trump
can force China to postpone the Made-in-China 2025 project!
What's the point? Postponement or not, why does it matter? What
good does it do to the people? That is not what the ruling elites
care; what they care is whether they can convince the electorate that
they are doing a good job. Although in fact, made-in-China 2025,
if achieved in time, can only benefit the average western consumer
with cheaper and better products; cheaper 5G, cheaper smartphones
and computers, better and cheaper electric cars, high-speed railway
at a cheaper price, cheaper and cleaner energy, perhaps even aircrafts.

Do we serious love the Boeing-Airbus monopoly? A monopoly in business is never good.

The whole world could benefit from made-in-China 2025 and we can cooperate. But unfortunately, western politicians and governments care more about the monopoly businesses than the average people. That's why the USA is trying to boycott Chinese products and block Chinese investments. They fabricate fake news in their favor, at the people's expense. Pure protectionism, paid by the consumers.

**And that's called democracy?**

Jiaojiang County Reading Village

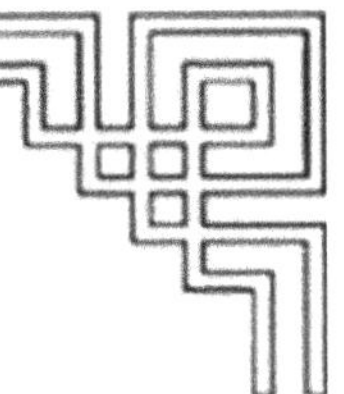



# 14.

# Censorship and Conflict Avoidance.

*#conflict #harmony #holism #balance #grant-face #censorship*
*#media #political-correct #democratic-dictatorship*

*The press is very much a reflection of individual freedom in a country. In Europe, the press is constantly pressured by an environment that encourages political correctness and one-sided ways of thinking. Even when ideologically they explore a variety of ideas, the quality and legitimacy of the European press is highly questionable. In China, a non-government funded press is very specific and straight forward regarding issues, just like how it is for the ordinary person with the Chinese culture.*

The media is one of the boldest and outlined outlets of connection between the government and the people. It speaks the words of the government to us and reflects the reactions of people back to the government. Western media is often filtered or biased in the transmission of ideas. It is important to discuss the implications and consequences of a two-sided media.

To a certain degree I have to agree with Eric C. Hendriks: China has a **culture of conflict avoidance**, which ensures that people avoid discussions — even on topics that are not politically sensitive. As a result, both Chinese journalists and their audience are not set to practise discussion and arguing.[47]

China doesn't avoid the discussion, but the exchange of ideas and opinion is made in an extremely respectful way. Dozens of think tanks, not just in Beijing but all over China point to thousands of issues in an amazingly straightforward way. They come up with propositions, and, following on from this, laws are proposed with an almost scientific methodology.

Discussion and argument are approached very differently in China

---

47   Eric C. Hendriks, "Echte diversiteit slaat je in het gezicht", *Doorbraak*, 29.12.2018
https://doorbraak.be/echte-diversiteit-slaat-je-in-het-gezicht/

compared to the West. It's straightforward, using facts and figures and scientific methods — and it always has harmony in its intention, ensuring that the opponents' feelings are not hurt.

**Holism** (Zhěngquánguān整全观 everything is connected, nothing exists in itself) and **balance** (yīn yáng 阴阳) are two of the most common ideas.

The whole of China, not just the government but also the ordinary Chinese, strives for 和谐社会 (héxié shèhuì) a **harmonious society**. Wen Jiabao, China's former prime minister, a major promoter of balance and harmony in Chinese society and in China's foreign relations, spoke of héxié shèhuì in almost every speech. If he went to visit a village or a city in the traditional west of China, you could set your watch by it: "我 希望 (wǒ xīwàng) I hope ..." and then something about the héxié shèhuì, social harmony.

**Grant face** (面子 liú miànzi). In China, it is considered a normal manner to show respect and praise each other in the presence of others. Suffering loss of face (失 面子 shī miànzi) is many times worse in China than in the West.

**There is more censorship in Europe than in China.**
There's no real freedom of the press in Europe:

Legally, freedom of the press is 'absolute' in Europe. If a publication mentions a *responsible publisher*, all opinions may be disseminated. Preventive government censorship is forbidden, press crimes should even be settled before the High Court. That's the theory.

Officially, there's no cloud in the sky. So, does that means there's nothing to worry about? Not really: freedom of thinking in Europe is still limited by formal censorship, self- or auto-censorship, influencing, state subsidies, political correctness and the one-sided thinking pattern of many journalists.

**People in Europe don't dare to speak openly their opinion.**

One could not express his opinion on certain topics or only with caution freely, said 78 percent of the Germans recently in an Allensbach survey[48], a good two-thirds (69%) expressed themselves in a Saxony survey by Infratest (Similar to MDR). In January 2019, handball star Stefan Kretzschmar caused a stir with his statement: "We have no freedom of expression in the true sense."

Europeans want to be colourful, tolerant and cosmopolitan. But when it comes to freedom of opinion, fun stops quickly! First and foremost, the refugee issue is one of the most sensitive topics for the vast majority of respondents, followed by statements of opinion on Muslims and Islam.

Political scientist Werner Patzelt also sees it that way. "Of course, you can express your opinion freely. However, one has to reckon with social follow-up costs, which can be very high. "Many, therefore, prefer to keep their opinions silent before speaking. While this pleases those who want to silence unwanted political positions, they vote on election day, namely by politically 'unwelcome' voting behaviour."

---

48  Prof. Dr. Renate Köcher, "Grenzen der Freiheit", *Institut für Demoskopie Allensbach in der Frankfurter Allgemeinen Zeitung,* 23.05.2019.
https://www.ifd-allensbach.de/fileadmin/user_upload/FAZ_Mai2019_Meinungsfreiheit.pdf

## State aid

In Europe, most of the mainstream media, including TV and radio are heavily subsidized. In Belgium for example, the VRT (Vlaamse Radio- en Televisieomroeporganisatie), the national state channel, receives 290 million euros annually, the newspapers and magazines another 400 million. Wouldn't it be much better (and more democratic) to give every citizen a kind of 'mediacheque'[49] so that they can decide for themselves how to spend that money?

In China, on the other hand, neither CCTV (the national TV with 45 channels), nor the press (2200 different newspapers) or internet media receive any financial support from the state.

## Political correctness

This is a huge problem throughout the whole of Western Europe. When it comes to domestic issues, some European readers are able to make critical judgements about what the media presents to them. The situation is slightly different for foreign subjects. Some readers, especially those who regularly consult foreign media, can also critically assess reports about neighbouring countries. But with regard to non-European subjects, the vast majority unquestionably swallow what is presented to them by the politically correct media in the US, Britain, Germany, France, … Many, almost all, well-educated citizens have no idea how different the rest of the world is from what they read in our mainstream media. Too many people debate about situations in Brazil, Russia, South Africa or China, never having been there and never having consulted media from those countries

49 Tom Cochez, "Mediacheque voor elke burger" *Apache*, 08.09.2014.
https://www.apache.be/2014/09/08/mediacheque-van-400-euro-voor-elke-burger/

themselves. Old clichés are being reheated and served again and again.

All my business or personal acquaintances – all of them! –, and all my family members who came to visit me in China, were stunned by what they saw, surprised that China is so different from the image they gathered from the Western media. Some felt quite misled by the media and were angry about it.

The totally different language and culture are of course significant barriers, but that should not be an excuse for the Western media: if they strive for quality, they owe it to their readers to go and find out their stories locally, in the local language.

## Taboos

As far as domestic issues are concerned, there are so many taboos in the Western media that there is hardly anything substantial left that is worth reporting. Criticizing islam is such a taboo, even after all the bloody attacks. Disorder in European capitals, criticism of the climate hype… The list of taboos is endless, — so many subjects that readers cannot reach.
Cultural hegemony at its finest, Antonio Gramsci could not have asked for a better example. [50]

## Auto-censorship and self-censorship

In addition to deep-rooted political correctness in European media, there is an ingrained system of self-censorship. New journalists are initiated quickly and efficiently into the system. Whoever wants to

---

50 "Cultural Hegemony," *Wikipedia, The Free Encyclopedia*, 20.10.2019
https://en.wikipedia.org/wiki/Cultural_hegemony

colour outside the lines, is quickly made aware where the boundaries lie. Harassment, dismissal or outright intimidation that they'll find themselves out of work is not unusual for those who do not follow the editorial vision.

**Formal censorship**

The Great Firewall (Golden Shield Project 金盾工程; jīndùn gōngchéng) blocks 57 words, phrases and names in most search engines in China. Some of them can still be found with Baidu or Sogou. [51] 52 foreign websites are currently being blocked, including Google, YouTube, Facebook and paedophilia and porn websites. [52] The official reason for blocking Google and Facebook is that these big American giants refuse to put their servers (with the private data of their Chinese users) in China. Perhaps the main reason is that in this way China protects its own Baidu and Youku-Tudou from competition with Western companies.

In addition, sporadic messages are removed from Sina Weibo (the Chinese Microblogging / Facebook).
**Formal Chinese internet censorship is technical and simplistic and is therefore not half as effective as Western informal self- or auto censorship.** All Western companies and most Chinese students use a VPN (virtual private network, usually encrypted) so that they have unlimited access to the whole internet.

In Europe, formal censorship is limited to blocking paedophilic websites in addition to the restrictions built in by Google and other search engines.

51  "List of Blacklisted Keywords in China", *Wikipedia, The Free Encyclopedia*, 20.10.2019 https://en.wikipedia.org/wiki/List_of_blacklisted_keywords_in_China
52  "Websites blocked in mainland China", *Wikipedia, The Free Encyclopedia*, 20.10.2019 https://en.wikipedia.org/wiki/Websites_blocked_in_mainland_China

## Quality

The quality of the European press is miserable. Almost all non-European news is blindly copied from other, mostly American sources, including factual inaccuracies, incompleteness and distortions. It is well known that a very large majority of journalists have left or centre-left views. More than 70% spend their days primarily in the editorial newsrooms. No newspaper has a journalist who is born in Asia or speaks Chinese.

The heavy subsidies given to the media by governments are without conditions for quality. It is therefore not surprising that, despite all of that money, there's zero improvement. [53]

## Overestimation, haughtiness, arrogance

Unfortunately, almost all media outlets suffer from a collective ailment of pedantic arrogance. Now that the village pastor and teacher have lost their influence and authority, they believe they should take over that role. Cathrine Gyldensted's 'constructive journalism' ensures that facts and figures in the regime media — the mouthpieces of the European governments — are always followed by an 'interpretation' so that the silly viewer or reader is guided in the right direction!
Foreign topics are discussed as if Europe is still significant on the world stage today.

In the Chinese media it's slightly different. When it comes to foreign news items, journalists are careful not to be overbearing. Modesty is the norm in China. When I read the Chinese press, I always think:

---

53 "Belgische mediasteun leidt tot slechtere kranten", *Apache*, 29.10.2015.
https://www.apache.be/2015/10/29/belgische-mediasteun-leidt-tot-slechtere-kranten/

be a little prouder of what has been achieved in China over the last
30 years; mention without anxiety that in China, many things are
better organized than in Europe!

## Influence and manipulation

The political and industrial establishment holds the media in its grip.
The generous influence of the OSF (Open Society Foundation) is felt
everywhere, not just in the media but in many social organizations.
With almost inexhaustible resources, the OSF[54] can exert pressure
subtly but very effectively everywhere.

In China, some time ago, there was a large-scale campaign (mainly
by journalists, but also by a number of politicians) against the
influence on the media by the GAPP (General Administration of
Press and Publication) on the media. China Daily, in particular, was
very sharp in its coverage of the GAPP's transgressions.

On Chinese social media there was a hype when the Ministry of
Culture established a Sina Weibo account. In more than 150000
responses, they were accused of influencing the media. [55] For
instance, shortly before, they had issued an advice not to have lesbian
or gay characters in soap operas. I can't even imagine a similar
action on Facebook or WhatsApp in which European citizens, in
the same strong terms, rage against political correctness in the
mainstream media.

<hr>

54  "OSF Open Society Foundation", Wikipedia, The Free Encyclopedia, 20.10.2019.
https://en.wikipedia.org/wiki/Open_Society_Foundations
55  Manya Koetse, "Ministry of Culture Weibo Account Controversy" What's on Weibo,
24.10.2015
http://www.whatsonweibo.com/ministry-of-culture-weibo-account-controversy/

## To conclude:

All the above, summarizing the various limiting factors for freedom of thought in two pie charts. In Europe and in China:

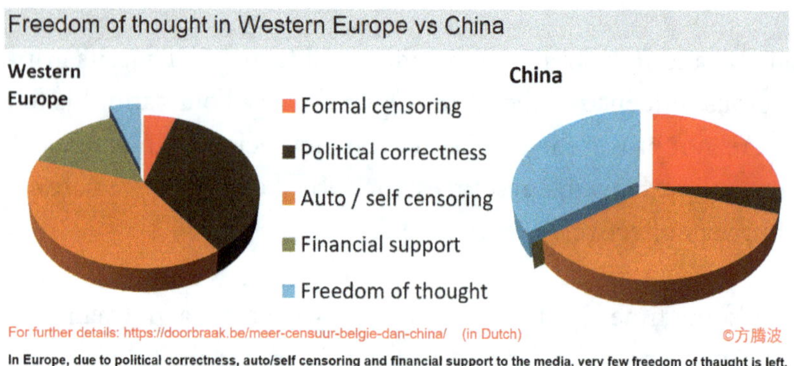


*Fig. 18 Freedom of thought in Western Europe vs China*

Longshang Books Cafe

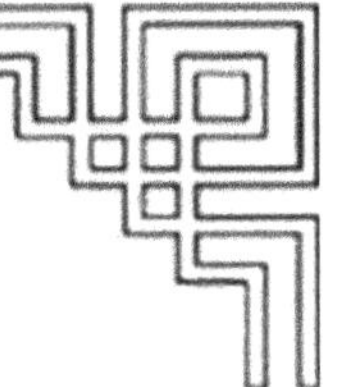



# 15.

# All Politics is Local.

*#politics #local #democratic–dictatorship*

This chapter is important to discuss due to the role of "We the people". Per-haps the most sworn by statement in China by politicians and leaders. Being a public servant is one of the major factors that separates corrupt and well-run countries. Discussing what it means to be a public servant and how a country can keep giving birth to them is an essential task in every country.

The saying goes that Western politicians can't succeed or survive without the electoral support of their local voters. But in these days of mass media marketing, a few seconds on TV, a witty, sharp statement in prime time during the evening news brings much more votes than a social, industrial or infrastructure project in the local township.

In China however, the first sentence of the first article of the first chapter of the *Constitution of The People's Republic of China* clearly states:
"The People's Republic of China is a socialist state under **the people's democratic dictatorship** led by the working class and based on the alliance of workers and peasants."[56]

Basically, that's not so different from "We the people" in the American constitution.

---

56 "people's democratic dictatorship" in Chapter 1, Article 1 of The Constitution of the People's Republic of China 20.10.2019
http://en.people.cn/constitution/constitution.html

All politicians should adhere to it; they have to behave as servants, as slaves of the people. It is not a trivial sentence in the constitution, it is the essence of daily life in China. It became quite clear to me during my first few weeks in China. As a Westerner, to see the 'servant' attitude of officials, police, public administration workers and politicians was remarkable. I never noticed this attitude among politicians in Western countries.

Chinese politicians have to gain their support from the people in a whole different way.



In China, I have met many dedicated politicians.
Dedicated, honest politicians? Sounds crazy, right?
Because most of Western politicians are opportunists, it follows that all politicians, all over the world must be opportunists. But this is not the case. It is difficult for Westerners to comprehend that, in China, officials and politicians are so highly committed and have real integrity.

China's tradition was to rule by morality. History proved it didn't work, so it was necessary to build a society ruled by law. Even when it is very hard; and sometimes, facing obstacles or turnaround, China will never give up! Thanks for the hard work in law industry there will be more justice to the people and more progress to the country!<sup>57</sup>

**古人的智慧，今天的幸福**

Gǔrén de zhìhuì, jīntiān de xìngfú

**The wisdom of the ancients is the welfare of youth.**

The Yellow Emperor Classics

57  Ye Mao, "Rule by Morality or Rule by Law?" in an email to me, 10.07.2019

Shanghai Tower 52nd Floor
Duoyun Bookstore

# 16.

# Petitioning and Opinion Polls.

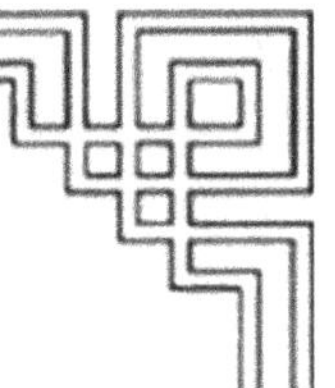

*#petitioning #discontent #flying-magistrates #public opinion
#polls #messageboard #MBLL*

*In China, the government is very adamant on hearing the voices of the people. Whether it is through polls, surveys, calls or the internet; people of China must be heard and listened to. This level of communication leads to cultural growth and law advancements. Chinese officials understand that the feeling of empowerment for Chinese people is very significant to how happy they feel in the environment.*

How well the voice of the people is communicated to the government is a very grand yet meaningful matter. Arguably the most impactful factor for a caring government is to hear feedback. However, it is not only important for a government to try and hear the feedback, but it is also about the method in which this task is done.

## Discontent[58]

Discontent in China is a constant and ever-present theme. How many economies in the world can claim to have an absolutely contented populace? Even when China had nothing, its people managed to eke out a living. Chinese people have become extremely good in finding opportunities despite conditions that many in the West would think hopeless.

The Chinese word for managing discontent is 疏导 shūdǎo. This is a compound word. 疏 means to unblock. 导 means to guide.

---

58  Richard Li, "Discontent in China" in a message to me, 15.02.2019

## China's ancient petitioning system[59]

Petitioning is a custom which has its origins in China's imperial past.

The idea was this: if a local official behaved intolerably, the people would go to the imperial capital and make an appeal to an imperial official, or in some cases, even to the emperor himself. The petitioners would lay out their case, explain the rationale for their appeal and ask for a senior official or the emperor to make a judgment.

This could be very dangerous: what would happen if the senior official or emperor sided with the local official, and ordered that all the petitioners be executed? For this reason, it was, at that time, considered a very risky strategy. In the TV series and detective stories of Judge Dee and Judge Bao, they were 'flying' magistrates who represented the emperor, which was why local officials all had to kowtow before them.

That was during the imperial era. Today, there's the internet and the Message Board for Local Leaders (MBLL, 'difang lingdao liuyanban').

The petitioning method continues to the present day. People still go to Beijing to complain. But during Hu Jintao's presidency, **local** officials sometimes went to train and bus stations to prevent petitioners from boarding trains. There were even a few cases where petitioners made it to Beijing and were kidnapped by corrupt local officials and taken back to their villages![60] Going to Beijing to impeach local politicians was considered to be a serious violation of the authority of Beijing central government.

---

59  Paul Denlinger, "China's Ancient Petitioning System" *in a message to me*, 16.02.2019
60  Paul Denlinger, "Petitioning in China" *in a message to me*, 15.02.2019

Xi Jinping has tried to modernize the petitioning system.[61] Also, as part of his "Tigers and Flies" anti-corruption war, he has strengthened the authority of the Party Discipline Committee of the CPC's Central Committee. They act as 'flying' magistrates or judges, sent out to the provinces to hunt down and remove corrupt local officials.

**How Beijing embraces public opinion to govern.[62]**

Puzzled by 'authoritarian resilience' in China after the 'third wave' of democratization in the late 20th century, scholars began to delve deeper into how the CPC fortified its power by tolerating public participation in politics. In this vein, the CPC came to embrace the internet as a tool to both improve governance and enhance control, particularly through the collection and analysis of online public opinion.

A fast-growing but under-studied case of this phenomenon is the **Message Board for Local Leaders** (MBLL, 地方领导留言板 dìfāng lǐngdǎo liúyánbǎn). Run by People's Daily Online (PDO) and also accessible via a dedicated app and through WeChat, the MBLL lets netizens leave public messages for provincial, city, and county governments, which can either ignore the message or respond publicly.[63]

---

61 "Petition Process is Made Easier", 13.03.2017
http://www.chinadaily.com.cn/china/2017-03/13/content_28527737.htm
62 "National Netizen Message Reply Processing Index Report", *The People's Daily Public Opinion Monitoring Office*, 23.09.2016
http://www.peopleyun.cn/index.php?m=content&c=index&a=show&catid=29&id=2
63 "The Message Board for Local Leaders (MBLL, difang lingdao liuyanban)" *People's Daily Online (PDO)*, 20.10.2019
http://liuyan.people.com.cn/index.html

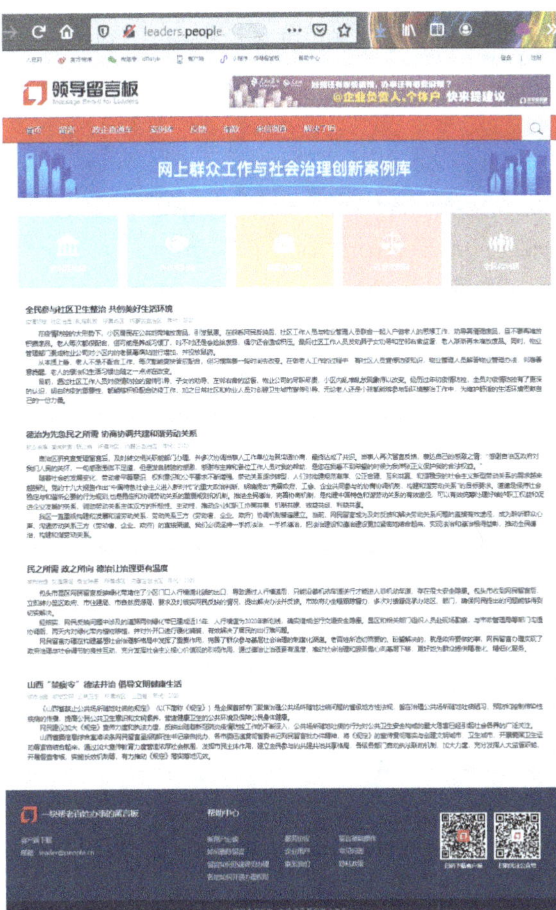

*Fig. 19 Screenshot of the Message Board for Local Leaders*

People's Daily Online says the platform aligns with Xi Jinping's call in April 2016 to the cadres:

We must learn to follow the mass line through the internet and understand what the people think and hope, collect good ideas and suggestions and actively respond to netizens' concerns.

Xi Jinping

Xi issued this order to get online 'shàngwǎng lìng' because, as he put it, "public opinion is online."

Established in 2006, the Message Board for Local Leaders had published a total of 1737962 messages by the end of April 2019, of which *66.4% had received public replies* from local governments. The interest in the site appears to have surged recently, with the total number of official responses in the first half of 2019 already 50000 more than the total for 2018. From January to April 2019, the 384631 messages posted by netizens garnered a response rate of 78.2%, up from 57.6% in April 2016.

**The MBLL (Message Board for Local Leaders)** is *surprisingly transparent*, allowing any viewer to see all the messages and responses for each local government. In aggregate this data points towards a positive correlation between response rate and message volume, implying a virtuous cycle of interaction between the government and the governed. The five provinces that account for over half of all messages and replies – Henan, Sichuan, Anhui, Gansu, and Shaanxi – also have five of the seven best response rates nationwide.

**The types of messages vary.** Issues such as wage arrears, dilapidated neighborhoods and forced land seizures (chāiqiān) are fairly common on the MBLL, as a sizeable share of messages come from rural farmers and lower-income suburbanites. Research suggests that official responses are more likely if the message was from a local resident, expressed collectively, focused on a single issue, and closely related to economic growth.

# Types and Topics of MBLL Messages:

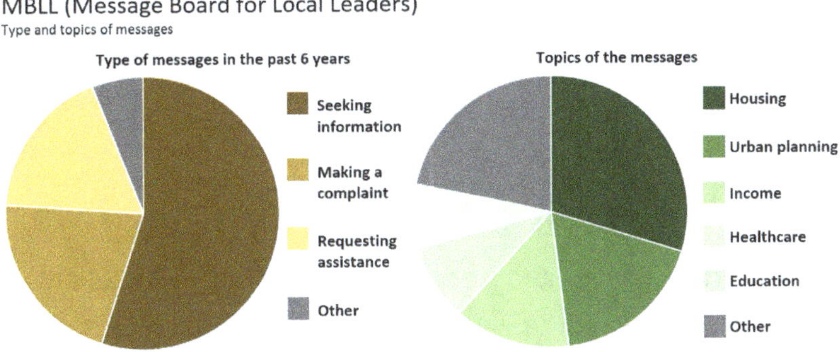


*Fig. 20 MBLL Type of topics of the messages*

## Empowerment:

The MBLL may have empowered Chinese citizens to voice their problems, but has it actually improved local governments' performance of local governments? A recent study in the *Governance* journal found that, from 2008 to 2013, city governments with a higher number of MBLL messages were not only inclined to devote significantly more space to social welfare in their annual work reports but also tended to substantively improve coverage of the dìbǎo, the universal basic income with Chinese characteristics.

This finding suggests that the MBLL does significantly improve local governance and improve the citizens' approval of the government. People's Daily Online claims that in 2018 over half of the MBLL users were satisfied with the reply they received. The success rate may explain why twenty-six of the provincial governments have established official procedures for collating, analyzing and responding to MBLL messages.

Most Common Keywords
in MBLL Messages in 2018[64]

*Fig. 21 Common Keywords in MBLL Messages*

**The MBLL's effectiveness** and its efficient user interface are likely key reasons why it is more popular than other online channels for citizen feedback. One such alternative is another PDO-operated site called "Conversations with Official Microblogs," which since July 2014 has recorded official responses to citizen complaints made to these microblogs. That site has registered a total of only 51800 netizen inquiries and 4601 replies, for an abysmal response rate of 8.9%. While other 'e-participation' initiatives have been popular -40% of petitions (xinfang) were filed online in 2016 - the MBLL is the only public, nationwide platform of its kind.

**There are limits to the MBLL,** of course, it is subject to the same redlines that apply to the rest of the Chinese internet. PDO deletes *forbidden* content. MBLL censorship targets politically *charged* messages but not those about *personal matters* or *local policy issues*. Because PDO is a central agency and not captive to local interests, local governments are more likely to respond to complaints made public on the MBLL than those received via the non-public online feedback portals that many localities now operate. *It is one of the ways, Xi Jinping want to incite local politicians to take up grassroots issues.*

The MBLL becomes an increasingly effective means to resolve low-

---

64  Holly He, "Most Frequent Keywords", *People's Daily Online*, 20.10.2019. http://leaders.people.com.cn/GB/178291/218130/425289/index.html

level policy issues. Its user base will likely continue to grow. The platform (or similar mobile apps) could well become an important fixture of Chinese governance in an age when more than 800 million Chinese are daily online.

The MBLL shows how technology can liberate. The platform enables Chinese netizens to interact directly with local governments to address real-life problems. On the other hand, the platform allows the government to solidify its control over society by *resolving grassroots conflicts and promoting social stability.*

## Opinion Polls

Recently, Xi Jinping has encouraged all institutes and researchers once again to conduct even more polls, so to have a much better contact with the real needs and concerns of the Chinese people.

The efficiency of the Chinese political system is breath-taking.

## Beijing Polls Residents on 'Uncivilized Behaviors' [65]

A government survey asks people living in the Chinese capital to identify 10 undesirable actions from a list of 20 and vote on possible punishments. In an effort to civilize the city, authorities in Beijing have issued a survey seeking residents' opinions on desirable versus undesirable behaviors - along with suitable punishments for the latter.

On-line surveys, usually remaining open to the public for 20 days, collect responses from the public, serving as the basis for future policies.

<hr>

65  Tang Fangxi, "Beijing Polls Residents on 'Uncivilized Behaviors'", *Sixth Tone*, 06.08.2019
https://www.sixthtone.com/news/1004398/beijing-polls-residents-on-uncivilized-behaviors

Participating residents are asked to select 10 out of 20 "uncivilized behaviors" - including spitting in public, petty vandalism, and cutting in line - that they believe are most deserving of punishment. Here's a closer look at five more distasteful deeds included on the list:

## Boisterous square dancers

To China's city-dwelling denizens, groups of retirees in matching outfits occupying public spaces and dancing in perfect synchrony are a common sight, especially during the waning hours of the day. But this seemingly benign pastime has also been criticized as a source of noise pollution, with some residents complaining about the blaring music disturbing their otherwise tranquil households.

In February 2017, the Beijing government announced that square dancing troupes found to be disturbing their neighbors would receive formal warnings — or even fines of up to 500 yuan (EUR 64) in the case of repeat offenders. Some creative communities have coped with the problem by issuing headphones to the dance groups, turning their evening plaza prances into silent discos.

## Sun's out, guts out

One of the most fascinating fashion phenomena in China can be observed each summer in sweltering cities, where men's shirts seem to rise along with the mercury to expose ample paunches.

In July, authorities in Shandong followed in the footsteps of another city, Tianjin. They announced that they would be cracking down on the so-called 'Beijing bikini', with punishments ranging from verbal warnings to public shaming.

Now, Beijing appears to be mulling whether its own namesake fashion trend should be covered up for good.

## Who let the dogs out… unleashed?

Dog ownership is on the rise in China, yet many pet owners are less than diligent when it comes to using a leash. According to a recent survey, Beijing authorities are considering punishing people who don't clean up after their pooches or keep them leashed in public.

Rabies is a major public health concern in China, where 12 to 16 million people are vaccinated against the virus each year. As such, some people don't take kindly to unleashed dogs — or to being chastised for not using leash. Last November, a dog owner in Shanghai punched a woman who had used her foot to shoo away his unleashed dog. And in July, police detained a man in Guangdong province for beating a golden retriever to death after the unleashed animal attacked and killed his poodle.

## Clean plate, clean conscience

As anyone who's ever eaten a large, family-style meal the country can tell you, Chinese people's eyes tend to be larger than their stomachs. But that may change some day, with Monday's survey listing wasting food as a potential uncivilized behavior.

In 2013, a Beijing-based nonprofit launched a conservation-minded campaign called 'Clear your plate.' Today, the campaign's page on microblogging platform Weibo has over 60000 followers and boasts dozens of photos of people showing off their spotless dishes.

The campaign exists for good reason. According to a 2018 study by the World Wide Fund for Nature, the average Chinese urbanite wastes around 12% of each meal, or 93 grams of food. Of the four cities surveyed, people in Chengdu wasted the most food at 103 grams per meal, while Beijingers wasted the least at 77 grams.

**Delinquent waste-sorters**

Beijing is slated to follow in Shanghai's footsteps and implement a compulsory citywide waste-sorting policy by 2020. For now, though, regulations are being rolled out on a smaller scale — in certain districts and public areas such as schools, hospitals, office buildings, and tourist sites, according to the city's deputy mayor. The Beijing Municipal Commission of Urban Management classifies waste into four categories: food waste, general waste, recyclables and hazardous materials.

As in Shanghai, authorities in the capital have opted for the carrot-and-stick approach to enforcing trash-sorting regulations. Residents who flout the rules may have their social credit scores docked or be fined up to 200 yuan, while those who sort their garbage correctly are rewarded with points that can be redeemed for household goods like toilet paper, seasonings, trash bags and kitchen knives.

**Social credit:**
It is expected that in all these public behavioral issues, the social credit system will assist to gradually eradicate behavior, unwanted by the majority of citizens.

Chongqing Real Estate
College Library

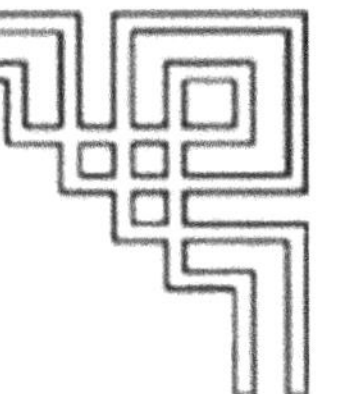

# The Autonomous Regions, a Whole Different world.

*#AR #Autonomous-Regions #power #democracy*

The following chapter explain how China found a perfect balance between modern perspectives and ancient traditions. It is difficult to maintain the integrity of an ancient culture while introducing new technologies, innovation, and ideas. China has used many different techniques both on the cultural and legal facets in order to achieve this beautiful harmony.

Within the People's Republic of China, the five autonomous regions (Tibet, Guangxi, Inner Mongolia, Ningxia, Xinjiang) are governed quite differently from the rest of China.[66]

As with most things inside a gigantic de facto empire, a country with several nations ruled by a central power, it is complicated. It is far worse in a place with a history of resistance to that rule, although the worst examples are technically provinces, not autonomous regions (Xinjiang and Tibet).

The most striking differences are at village level. This is because in the Deng era, the PRC experimented with democracy at the village level. President Jimmy Carter was an observer in this process. China didn't like it and refused to extend the idea to county, provincial or national level. But they have not tried to roll it back. Village officials

---

66  Lawrence Trevethan, "How do the autonomous regions in China function within the People's Republic of China?", Quora, 17.02.2019
https://www.quora.com/How-do-the-autonomous-regions-in-China-function-within-the-People-s-Republic-of-China-How-are-they-governed-differently-from-the-rest-of-China

compete for office and, with a single exception, *are never Communist Party members*! The single exception is one single show-village with a subsidy. There, the communists always win.

Village officials often defy county officials and go to jail leading protests - just to prove they are for the village! If it is in an autonomous region in a village, almost everyone is of a minority ethnic group. Their customs are respected. A day in jail is an excellent marketing technique for local elections. A technique, closely related to the 碰瓷 pèngcí "touch porcelain" culture.

When he was vice president, I met Hu Jintao in Southern China. He was traveling incognito and observing an outdoor choir event (raising money to build a church). For some reason, he assumed 'the white man' would know what was 'really' going on? He asked why people were donating to build a church, when for four years officials had been unable to get enough donations to build a bridge in the same place? [I didn't explain that the government should build bridges, not the local people. I did say: "people will donate to get what they want."] There was a South China Morning Post reporter in earshot who recognized him. The incident appeared as an item in the newspaper the following day. This was 1991 - when Hong Kong was still part of Britain and when the South China Morning Post was still a quality newspaper. Today, the SCMP is a western style tabloid.

At the national level, the only indication one sees is that a handful of delegates to the People's Congress are dressed in traditional instead of formal clothing. There is nothing like tribal police who are all members of the local ethnic group members and under control of a local government entirely run by that ethnic group. Quite the reverse, the PRC tends to trust police or soldiers from the region if there is any problem in an area.

And problems are normal: in the 1990s, massive riots happened at a rate of 400 times a year; today it is over 1000 times a year. The People's Armed Police have 6 SWAT organizations of battalion size - one for each region plus a national one - just if the local People's Armed Police Force cannot control a local riot. Now, the PAP has formally joined the PLA as part of the 2017 reorganization. It used to be basically run by province or autonomous region government. This police force is composed of divisions - most formerly Army infantry divisions.

Guangzhou Zhongshan Library

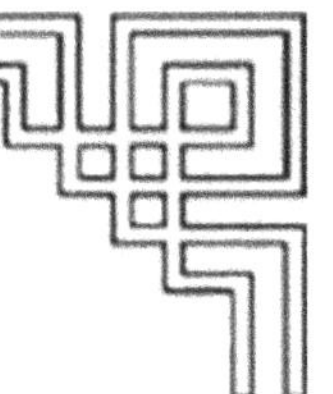

# Chapter
# 18.

# The Party.

*#Party #CPC #minor-parties #opposition #meritocracy #constitution*

*There are many different political parties operating and challenging each other in China. The strongest party currently being the Chinese Communist Party. However, Chinese policy and politics make sure that there is no barrier to entry. Many other up and coming parties are stating their case and also trying to serve the people within their own ideals. Each party has different steps for members to rise in the ranks, and as always; these steps are very selective and excruciating.*

Political parties are bound to exist in practically every country. For elections and democratic processes to work, everyone can not always be of an independent subset. Parties allow for likeminded individuals to appeal to their audience and share ideas with their peers. This makes it vital for the average person to understand parties, their function and variety.

China has nine political parties; the most overmastering is obviously the Chinese Communist Party. Founded in Shanghai in 1921 with only fifty-three members, it has now burgeoned to 89 million.

## The nine political parties in China:

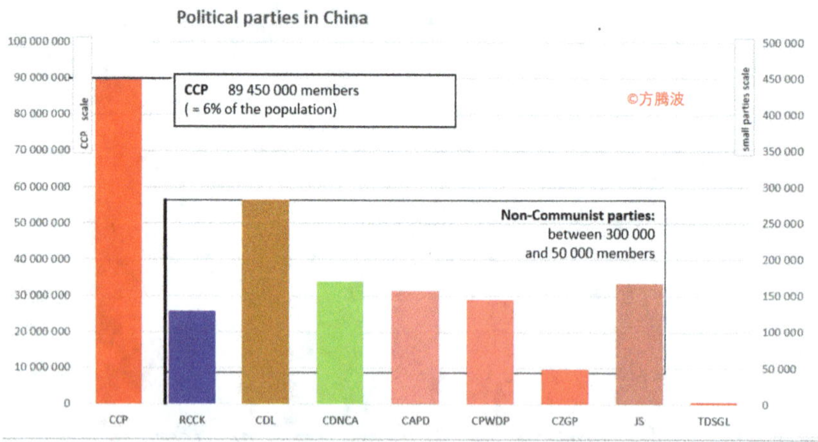


*Fig. 22 Political parties in China ©方腾波*

Not all politicians are Communist Party members: at the last
National People's Congress election, almost 30% of the members
were not CPC members.

Gòngchǎndǎng 共产党has been the name of the party since its
founding and it has always meant "Communist Party". "gong chǎn"
literally means "common property". The common English acronym
for the Chinese Communist Party is CPC.

The CPC's USP (unique selling proposition) is the 'dictatorship
of the people',[67] in great contrast to the 'mandate of heaven' of the
former emperors. Some people have attributed the Mandate of
Heaven to Xi Jinping. He himself has never claimed it. In practice,
however, he has the heavenly mandate, much more than most
emperors from bygone times. More than eighty percent of the
Chinese population supports him in the way he is managing the
country. No other president, prime minister, emperor or king ever
got such a high rating.

Chinese political parties are in no way comparable with western
political parties. They're much more like **service clubs**, Lions or
Rotary Club. The CPC's adage is "Serve the People" and their oath is
"I promise to bear the people's hardships first and enjoy the benefits
last". With their gifts and membership fees they contribute more
than CNY 10 billion per year to the welfare of China.

In **"The Party: The Secret World of China's Communist Rulers"**[68]
**Richard McGregor** delves deeply into China's inner sanctum for the

---

67 "people's democratic dictatorship" in Chapter 1, Article 1 of The Constitution of the
People's Republic of China 20.10.2019
http://en.people.cn/constitution/constitution.html
68  Richard McGregor, "The Party: The Secret World of China's Communist Rulers", *New
York, Harper, ISBN13: 9780061708770, 320 pages*, 08.06.2010.

first time, showing how the Communist Party works. Unfortunately, this book, published in June 2010 is hopelessly outdated. In the West, it is nevertheless still regarded as the bible, a standard reference work about the Communist Party of China.

In a more recent presentation on Youtube, Richard McGregor confirms that meritocracy within the Communist Party of China is measured with **KPI's** (Key Performance Indicator) in a "McKinsey & Co" way.[69]

In a conversation last December, a close friend, top-official within the Ministry of Commerce confirmed to me that **"the days of Guānxì and Máotái"** are over now, that 95% of the politicians and officials are promoted on their merits.

**The Constitution of the Communist Party of China.**
Revised and adopted at the 19th National Congress of the Communist Party of China on 24 October, 2017.[70]

**Organizational status of the CPC** [71]

The Party's local organizations, according to administration, are at three levels: province, city and county. Until now, province-level Party committees have been established in 31 provinces (autonomous regions, municipalities), city-level committees in 333 province-administrated cities (prefectures), and county-level committees in 2859 counties (cities, districts).

---

69   Richard McGregor, "Meritocracy within the CPC", *YouTube*, 20.10.2019.:
https://youtu.be/ym1d0ZScElk
70   "The Constitution of the Communist Party of China", 24.10.2017
http://www.china.org.cn/20171105-001.pdf
71   Liang Jun, Yao Chun, "Organizational Status of the CPC", *People's Daily Online*, 29.03.2013
http://english.cpc.people.com.cn/206972/206981/8188126.html

**The Party's grassroots organizations** refer to those established
within enterprises, rural areas, government offices, schools, scientific
research institutions, residential communities, social groups,
social intermediary agencies, PLA units and other lower-level
establishments. The Party Constitution mandates the establishment
of a Party committee in any organization that has more than three
full members of the Party.

Western labour unions and their representatives in companies in
Europe and the US are much more 'communist' with their unfeasible
demands than the work units - the CPC committees - in large
enterprises in China. The clashes between these two are shown
vividly in the movie *The American Factory*, with Fuyao owner Cao
Dewang trying to compromise between the two cultures during the
start-up of his new factory in Ohio, USA.

## Should the Communist Party change its name?

The Chinese Communist Party is a "Communist" Party. But it's also
a "Chinese" Party. Being "Chinese" meaning being pragmatic.[72]

So, bear in mind:

If there is something western people accuse the CPC of doing, that
serves no obvious beneficial purpose other than:

"Just Communism being evil"

"Because it's a fascism"

"Heavily censored police state"

"Anti-human in nature"

"Dictatorship sustaining itself"

then, it's probably fake news.

---

72 Mo Chen, "Are there many users paid by the Chinese Communist Party to spread the
Communist Party's propaganda on Quora?", Quora, 18.12.2018
https://www.quora.com/Are-there-many-users-paid-by-the-Chinese-Communist-Party-
to-spread-the-Communist-Party-s-propaganda-on-Quora

Will "hiring people to propagate communism on the internet" having any benefit to the CPC? No, not at all. Its name is, to be honest, rotten to core <u>in the English-speaking community</u>. To borrow the expression "beat a dead horse", this is the scenario where you'd be trying to "CPR (cardiopulmonary resuscitation) a dead horse".

More than often, I get comments and doubts from foreigners that look like this: "China isn't that bad but why can't the CPC change its name so we like it?"

It means if the CPC truly cares about its image in the west, it should be aware "Communism" is a hated, despised, and a hostile term, and try to change it. But it hadn't done that.

If I were to be hired to whitewash the CPC in the western media, I'd be banging my head trying to figure out this: Why is the CPC hiring people to build its image, while remaining using the most un-white-washable name in the west? I think it would've changed its name first, if it were severe. But it doesn't give two cares about what western people think of the CPC. Should the CPC change its name, just to make westerners happy?

**These are the general steps to join the Chinese communist Party:**

1.  Work or study at a place with the Party branch (党支部 dǎng zhībù). Try to work hard and keep a good relationship with your tutor or team leader.
2.  Hand in the application letter (入党申请书 rùdǎng shēnqǐng shū) to show that you want to join the Party. The letter should cover 3 items:
    1) CPC is a great Party

2) I want to join the Party

3) I am a qualified candidate.

3.  You will be asked to attend the lectures about the CPC (上党
    课 shàng dǎngkè) the board class. After each lecture, you should
    hand in an essay about how you feel or what you have learnt on
    the lecture. A party member will be assigned to be your mentor (
    介绍人 jièshào rén). The job of the mentor is to read your essays
    (but actually most of them don't) and talk to you regularly. After
    all lectures are finished, you have to take the exam on the history
    of CPC and critical political issues, events, conferences during
    the recent years.

4.  Hand in the essays regularly and keep in touch with your director.

5.  This step is crucial. Every period, usually half a year, the Party
    branch will select some candidates. These people will be
    developed as new party member.

6.  They will do a background check (外调 wàidiào) on the selected
    candidates. You will be invited to attend the discussion meeting
    about you. Your mentor's opinion is critical during this discussion.
    People, close to you will talk about you on that meeting. But you
    don't know who will be invited until the meeting begins.

7.  Hand in other necessary materials and attend some I-don't-
    know-what-for meetings or lectures.

8.  Finally, after taking the oath, you become a CPC member.
    The oath: "I am willing to join the CPC, advocate it, obey it,
    protect it, will be loyal to it forever, I am willing to sacrifice
    myself for it at any time, I will never betray the Party."

The fee for Communist Party membership is 2 to 3 % of your
monthly wage. On average, only 10% of the candidates get through
the selection process.

**Rising through the ranks of the Party.**[73]

General members of the CPC do not rise up in the ranks by election. Meritocracy does not mean election.

A CPC member can only rise through the rank by demonstrating merit in his/her respective fields, and then by appointment.

Even Xi himself wasn't elected, since you can't really call a 7-person committee an election. He was appointed by consensus. Election is not practiced within the ranks of CPC.

At the end of 2018, the Communist Party of China had 90.59 million members.[74]
Membership is still growing but at a slower rate than 5 years ago.[75] That's a deliberate choice to prevent too much opportunism creeping into the party ranks.

About 5 million CPC members, 6%, are party- and government staff. More than half of the CPC members have a college degree or above, 66% has a graduate degree, 25% has a PhD. With their 10%, the ethnic minorities are slightly over-represented in the party.

**Dao Tao, 10 years CPC member:**

73   Richard Li, "How effective, widespread, meritocratic, and transparent is the whole process in choosing the best-committed leadership?", *Quora*, 21.02.2019
https://www.quora.com/China-has-an-election-process-for-the-members-of-CCP-to-rise-up-the-levels-to-partake-in-government-how-effective-widespread-meritocratic-and-transparent-is-the-whole-process-in-choosing-the-best-committed
74   Chen Fei, "Membership of CPC tops 90 million", *China.org.cn*, 01.07.2019
http://www.china.org.cn/china/2019-07/01/content_74938199.htm
75   Minnie Chan, "Growth in Chinese Communist Party membership slows to decades low", *South China Morning Post*, 01.07.2016
https://www.scmp.com/news/china/policies-politics/article/1983762/growth-chinese-communist-party-membership-slows-decades

"I'm a 10 years CPC member, I don't feel much different from normal Chinese people. The major differences are:

1.  Party membership dues are 2% of my salary.

Every half year, I write a short summary about my political thoughts. Such as what I have learnt from the recent political events, if I have a new understanding about Communism.

Criticism and self-criticism. We organize an offline sync meeting to discuss about Socialism, Communism and Capitalism; and update our understanding.

Basically, I'm proud to be a member of CPC. I think most members are nice people, they are open minded."

**China is remarkably transparent about its officials**. All the Chinese officials' biography is consultable online via Chinavitae.com [76]

A more lively, interactive and user-friendly database with all the officials is at the MacroPolo website 'the Committee'. [77]

**The 'Tigers and Flies' action is still ongoing:** Last year, 13000 Party committees and primary Party organizations, 237 discipline inspection committees and 61000 Party members were found guilty of various infractions, according to a work report released in February 2019 by the Central Commission for Discipline Inspection. A newly revised regulation adds a new part that stipulates the

---

76  "Chinese Officials' Biography" 20.10.2019
http://www.chinavitae.com/research/
77  "The Committee" MacroPolo, 20.10.2019
https://macropolo.org/digital-projects/the-committee/

detailed investigation procedure after officials are alleged to have committed infractions.[78]

**One day, the Communist Party will die:** Mao Zedong, at the Commemoration of the Twenty-eighth Anniversary of the Communist Party of China, said: [79]

*"Like a man, a political party has its childhood, a youth, manhood and old age. The Communist Party of China is no longer a child or a lad in his teens but has become an adult. When a man reaches old age, he will die, and the same holds true of a party. For the working class, the laboring people and the Communist Party the question is not one of being overthrown but of working hard to create the conditions in which classes, state power and political parties will die out very naturally and mankind enters the realm of Great Harmony, dàtóng."*

Mao Zedong, 1949

---

78  "Zhang Yi, "Party Issues Regulation to Boost Cadres' Accountability", *China Daily*, 05.09.2019
https://www.chinadaily.com.cn/a/201909/05/WS5d704659a310cf3e35569c74.html
79  Mao Zedong, "On the People's Democratic Dictatorship", 30.06.1949
The Political thoughts of Mao Zedong

Beijing National Library of China

# 19.

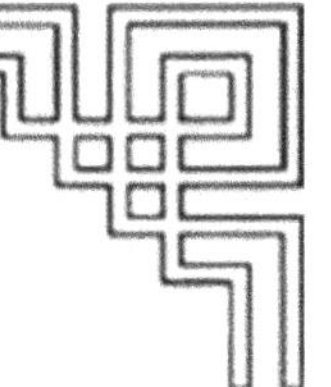

# Meritocracy, how it Works in Daily Life.

*#meritocracy #ability #integrity #cadres #selection #discipline*

*Governmental promotions and elections are incredibly selective and picky in China. These selections are often composed of various stages including tests, polls, history checks and interviews. Only the elite and perfect candidates make it to the top given the prominence of their role in society. This is why many politicians are not only intelligent but also adequately able in regards to their roles and responsibilities.*

Every country has its own process for electing officials. Whilst it is not particularly impactful directly about how officials get elected and chosen; subconsciously this is the process that determines the integrity and efficiency of governmental personnel. China has a pervasive and selective process which is outlined in this chapter.

## The harsh selection process of officials and political leaders.[80]

The process of choosing the President and General Secretary is the same at all levels, but the criteria become more stringent as cadres rise in rank. Here's the touching story of provincial official Zhao BingBing [81], describing the process at her level:

"I was promoted in 2004 through my department's internal competition (30 percent on written exam results, 30 percent on interviews and public speaking, 30 percent on public opinion of my work and 10 percent on education, seniority, and my current position) and became the youngest deputy division chief. In 2009, Liaoning Province (population 44 million), announced in the national media an open selection of officials. Sixty candidates met

---

80  Godfree Roberts, "How does the Chinese government decide who succeeds the outgoing President and General Secretary?", *Quora*, 04.05.2019. https://www.quora.com/How-does-the-Chinese-government-decide-who-succeeds-the-outgoing-President-and-General-Secretary

81  Daniel Bell and Zhao Bingbing, "The China Model, A Conversation between a Communist and a Confucian" *Princeton Press*, 01.05.2013. http://assets.press.princeton.edu/releases/m10418-2.pdf

the qualifications, the top five of whom were invited for further interviews. Based on their test scores (40 percent) and interview results (60 percent), the top three were then appraised. The Liaoning Province organizational department sent four appraisers who spent a whole day checking my previous records. Eighty of my colleagues were asked to vote - more than thirty of whom were asked to talk with the appraisers about my merits and shortcomings. Finally, they submitted the appraisal report to the provincial Standing Committee of the CPC for review.

In principle, the person who scored the highest and whose appraisals were not problematic would be promoted. However, because my university major, work experience and previous performance were the best fit for the position, I was finally appointed as department chief of the Liaoning Provincial Foreign Affairs Office even though my overall score was second best. The government also discriminates positively in promoting women. Before the official appointment, there was a seven-day public notice period during which anybody could report to the organization department concerns about my promotion. I didn't spend any money during my three promotions; all I did was study and work hard and do my best to be a good person.

In 2013, thanks to an exchange program, I worked temporarily in the CPC International Department. The system of temporary exchanges offers opportunities to learn about different issues in different regions and areas like government sectors and SOEs. In a famous quote Chairman Mao said, "Once the political lines have been clearly defined the decisive factor will be the cadres [trained specialists]." So, the CPC highly values organizational construction and the selection and appointment of specialists. There is a special department managing this work, The Organization Department, established in 1924. The department is mainly responsible for the macro management of the leadership and the staff, their cooperation, including the management system, regulations and laws, human resource system reforms - planning, research and direction -, as well as proposing suggestions on the leadership change and the appointment of cadres. In addition, it has the responsibilities of training and supervising cadres. The cadre selection criteria are: a person must have 'both ability and moral integrity and the latter should be prioritized'. The evaluation of moral integrity focuses mostly on service to the people, self-discipline, integrity and loyalty to the Party. Based on different levels and positions, the emphases of evaluation are also different. For intermediate and senior officials, emphasis is on their persistence in faith and ideals, political stance and coordination with the central Party. High-level cadres are measured against great politicians and, among them, experience in multiple positions is very important."

The track records of a thousand top politicians, available online [82], are impressive. Most, like Xi Jinping, started their political careers as manual laborers in dirt-poor villages in the late sixties and doubled the incomes of the people they governed, got PhDs and ran huge provinces, Fortune 500 corporations, universities or space programs. As they advanced, they spent sabbaticals on the leafy, lake-studded campus of The Academy of Governance (CAG, the former CNSA) where they met the world's leading thinkers and critiqued policies with senior policymakers.

---

82  "The Committee", *MacroPolo*, 20.10.2019
https://macropolo.org/the-committee/

The process of choosing the President and General Secretary is the same at all levels, but the criteria become more stringent as cadres rise in rank.

**Today, China is a full Meritocracy.** *The days of "Guānxì and Máotái" are over now, 95% of the politicians and officials are promoted on their merits.*

a top-official within the Ministry of Commerce

Suzhou Humble Administrator Garden

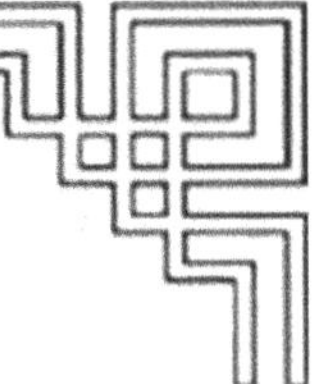



# 20.

# Trias Politica, Separation of Power, Checks and Balances.

*#Trias-Politica #separation-of-power #checks&balances*

A government is usually made of many parts which are responsible for decisions, legislations, plans and executions of ideas. Whether these parts are interconnected as one body or separate, depends on the country. It is important to discuss the disadvantages or shortcomings of a divided and singular government. China is making great strides in doing all that can be done in ensuring cohesion and long-term coherence within government plans.

## Trias Politica, checks and balances and separation of powers.

### In China:

Last year, Zhou Qiang (周强) Chief Justice and President of the Supreme People's Court of China said: "[China's courts] must firmly resist the western idea of 'constitutional democracy', 'separation of powers' and 'judicial independence'. These are erroneous western notions. We must raise our flag and show our sword to struggle against such thoughts. We must not fall into the trap of western thoughts and judicial independence."

### In the West:

The at first sight noble intentions of the Trias Politica in many Western countries' constitution are gradually eroded. Today, with the power shift from representative democracy to the mainstream media, Checks and Balances are reduced to a political theatre. Often,

the Separation of Power is only used as a fig-leave for not to take
the action, required or requested by a majority of the people. There
is no real trias politica in the West; the media, the political and
the judiciary are so strongly connected to the economic power that
mutual influence cannot be avoided.

China has valid reasons for <u>not</u> having formal Checks and Balances.
There is a separation between the Party and the Government,
but not in the same way as the Separation of Powers in Western
constitutions. The Chinese political system doesn't require a Trias
Politica because, as per the Chinese constitution, the whole political
system is the 'slave of the people'.

Dedicated politicians, committed to their 'civil-servant' mission, don't
need a formal separation of powers to assure they will not abuse
their power.
The Chinese legal system, up to 2012 infamous for meddling of local
politicians, has been cleared from such abuse after the Tigers and
Flies action. Globally, for enforcing contracts, it is now at rank 6 of
the most righteous and efficient juridical systems of the world.[83]

China might not have the Trias Politica in the constitution, it has
ensured the independence on another, much more efficient way:
in most courts and tribunals, there are cameras, not to guard the
defendant, but the judge. With life streaming on the social media,
judges have no other option than to make a judgment in accordance
with what people expect.

Foreign faith in Chinese courts is on the rise.[84]

---


83  "The World Bank - Doing Business Index", 20.10.2019
https://www.doingbusiness.org/en/data
84  "Foreign Faith in Chinese Courts is On The Rise", *China Daily*, 09.09.2019
https://www.chinadaily.com.cn/a/201909/09/WS5d75ac4ca310cf3e3556a6af_1.html

Recently, Luo Dongchuan, vice-president of the Supreme People's Court, ordered all judges who handle foreign-related disputes to improve the quality of trials and provide quicker and more convenient legal services for litigants.

Walking through the many beautiful gardens in Suzhou, one day, I stumbled upon the '**Humble Administrator Garden**'. Imagine such a name for a garden in a Western country!

方腾波

Nanjing Library

# 21.

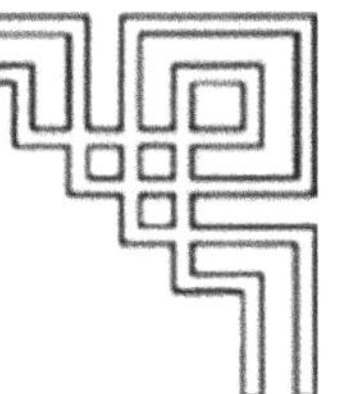

# Plum Blossoms in the Bitter Cold.

*#demographics #history #Nanjing-University
#academic #library*

*China is home to many educated and intelligent people. Stories like Mr. Fuson's show how even older generations cared deeply about education. Not only technical knowledge and innovation but also a good understanding of history is always appreciated in China. Chinese universities are very supportive in terms of costs and flexibility for their aspiring students.*

This chapter is important due to its ability to resonate with a humanly experience, with someone with strong opinions which are very different from the mainstream and the CPC viewpoints. This kind of dissent is perfectly accepted in China. Mr. Hu Fusun lectures at universities all over China, not only about his grandfather's history, but also about his politically controversial views. Mr. Hu's view is less of a commentary and more like a sit down with an experienced, well-educated citizen in China.

**An interview with Mr. Hu Fusun about his grandfather Hu Huanyong, the founder of the Hu-line:**

*Fig. 23 Interview with Mr. Hu Fusun on 23.11.2018 in Nanjing about his grandfather*

Frans Vandenbosch: Western media organizations are reporting
very negatively about China. I hope that through my efforts, I can
gradually change this situation.
I have been introduced to you by Mr. Yang. Mr. Yang is a friend
of mine in Belgium, I recommended Mr. Yang to be an actor on
national TV. This conversation with you is in preparation for writing
my second book. My book will make more progress next year. It will
be about grassroots politics in China. President Xi Jinping is a top-
level politician, so there are plenty of books about him. But my book
*Statecraft and Society in China* is about the situation of the ordinary
people. I want to get a better understanding of their political
concerns. What are they complaining about and how do they express
their dissatisfaction?

Mr. Hu Fusun:

Thank you, Mr. Fang, for your attention. I know that you're
from Belgium, in the heart of Europe. This is the report of our
conversation, arranged according to subject:

1.  My grandfather's family
2.  My grandfather's main experience
3.  Grandfather's main achievement and the Hu Huanyong line
4.  Considerations about the National Central University
5.  My family and work experience
6.  My understanding of Chinese society today

Fig. 24 Hu Huanyong stele

Fig. 25 Hu Huanyong stele unveiling on 01.01.2020

Fig. 26 The words "地理" (geography) and "胡焕庸" (Hu Huanyong) are written at the stele in the calligraphy of Hu Huanyong.

## 1. My grandfather's family.

My grandfather Hu Huanyong is a famous demographer in China. My grandfather was born in 1901. He lost his father in his childhood. His mother used her sewing to feed my grandfather. My grandfather was admitted to the Nanjing Normal School free of charge. After graduation, he went to study at the University of Paris, France. After returning to China, he taught at the National Central University and East China Normal University for a long time. On April 30, 1998, my grandfather died in Shanghai at the age of 98.

My grandparents had seven children and my father was the eldest son. I am the eldest grandson of the Hu family.

As for genealogy research, indeed many Chinese people do that. But our family doesn't. We do not have particular interest in genealogy. Everyone works and lives on their own. My grandfather's numerous materials, books and reports, everything I can find is saved as commemoration. We also donate some to the universities and public libraries. At the 110th anniversary of our grandfather's birthday in 2011, our descendants compiled a commemorative anthology about his life and achievements. The book is titled **Méihuā xiāng zì kǔhán lái** meaning: **'Plum blossoms from the bitter cold.'** For the first edition, only 300 books were printed. Many friends couldn't get one. Last year we printed another 200 copies. So now, I can hand over one to you, Mr. Fang. In the book, there are articles about the Hu line and population distribution. In total, my grandfather has written more than 400 books. I have a few books that were published during the Anti-Japanese War.

## 2. My grandfather's professional experience

After my grandfather returned from a study-tour in France in 1928, he was immediately hired by the National Central University as a professor of geosciences. Together with his teacher, Harvard University Doctor of Meteorology, Mr. Qi Kezhen, he set up the National Meteorological Observatory. In 1930 my grandfather became the first Dean of the Department of Geography of the National Central University. He also served as the dean of the whole Central University. In 1942 the Ministry of Education of the National Government hired professors (titled 'national professor') in two batches of 45 people. Hu Huanyong, my grandfather was one of them, who was also the only one in the field of geography [and anthropology]. He was one of the founders and served as the director and chairman of the Chinese Geography Society.

My grandfather was a member of the Kuomintang [85], as the
Kuomintang government required the president and famous
professors of the universities to be Kuomintang members. The
president of the National University and many professors at that
time were all Kuomintang members. But he has been a scientist all
his life. Chairman Jiang Zhongzheng once asked my grandfather
to abandon his professorship to take on important positions in the
Kuomintang party and the government. My grandfather disagreed.
At that time, academics were free to choose and often criticized the
government in their academic research reports.

After the Chinese Communist Party established a new political
power in Beijing in 1949, the National Central University was
renamed to Nanjing University and the status of my grandfather
changed significantly. My grandfather and eight other so called
'reactionary' professors at the Nanjing University were asked to go to
Beijing to review and explain their previous experience. There were
rumours that my grandfather was one of the six great agents left
by the Kuomintang. If that were true, he risked being executed. It
finally turned out to be slander. He was just a scientist, working on
scientific research and government projects that required university
research. But after the review, he was not only deprived of leadership
positions in the academic fields of Chinese geography, but also his
students (and a former student, a professor of geography at NCU)
also refused to allow my grandfather to teach at Nanjing University,
where he had worked for more than 20 years. The new government
also stipulated that he couldn't stay in Beijing, the capital city. He
was the only national-level professor in the geographic field. He
was one of the founders of the Chinese Geographical Society and
the chairman of the Chinese Geography Society. Many scientists

85  "Kuomintang KMT 国民党Guómíndǎng", *Encyclopedia.com*, 20.10.2019
https://www.encyclopedia.com/history/asia-and-africa/chinese-and-taiwanese-history/
kuomintang

in geography and meteorology circles underwent the same fate.
They were banned from the Institute of Geography of the Chinese
Academy of Sciences even if many scientists and professors in the
field of geology and meteorology were his students.

中国科学社等七学术团体在上海召开科学年会，图为大会主席台
右起：胡焕庸、卢于道、竺可桢、任鸿隽、翁文灏
1947 年 8 月 30 日摄于中央研究院礼堂

*Fig. 27 Opening of the academic year 30.08.1947 at the Chinese Academy of Sciences. From left to right: Weng Wenhao, Ren Hongjun, Zhu Kezhen, Lu YuRoa, Hu Huanyong.*

But then in 1950, the Huaihe River breached the dikes and flooded.
Most of the victims drowned in the north of the country. The
government asked my grandfather to participate in the management
of the Huaihe River flood. The project mobilized 2.5 million migrant
workers and 80% of the state's water-control funds. My grandfather
was responsible for designing water conservancy projects, guiding
the floodwaters into the sea and effectively controlling the Huaihe
River water damage.

In 1953, my grandfather came to teach at the newly established East
China Normal University in Shanghai. He couldn't do geography
research on his most familiar and beloved population geography. He
could only teach general geography such as ancient geography and
European geography. In this university, because of the new regime's
political movements, my grandfather was constantly censored,
criticized and ransacked. During the 'Cultural Revolution' that began

in 1966, he was repeatedly publicly criticized, then fired and forced
to sweep and repair roads. He was unable to read books for more
than a decade and could not do what he was best at. Being slandered
as a 'historical counter-revolutionary', he was arrested and jailed
for five years without any valid reason. The only lucky thing is that
he survived through hardships. After the Cultural Revolution, my
grandfather began to slowly resume research on population issues at
the age of 80.

In 1982, the Ministry of Education of the State Council
rehabilitated him and cancelled all the crimes imposed on my
grandfather in the past 30 years. But as he was over 80 years old,
this famous science's best working time had been eradicated. After
learning about my grandfather's ground-breaking research at the
East China Normal University, the United Nations Population
Fund provided 380 000 USD, a huge sum of money at that time,
right after the Cultural Revolution. Since then, the anthropology
division at the East China Normal University was managed by my
grandfather. With the rapid development, it is still one of the best
population research institutions in China.

After my grandfather's death in 1998, the People's Daily, a newspaper
of the Central Committee of the Communist Party of China,
issued an obituary. My grandfather was called a "famous geographer,
anthropologist, demographer, founder of contemporary Chinese
population geography... he has made outstanding contributions to
the development of human geography in China." [86] The Chinese
Communist Party, the Chinese government and the leading
scientists expressed their highest respect for him.

---

86   She Weiyi, "Hu Huanyong: father of China's population geography." *NCBI*, 15.08.1998.
https://www.ncbi.nlm.nih.gov/pubmed/12294257

# 3. Grandfather's main achievement and the Hu Huanyong line

Grandfather was not only a geographer but also a famous demographer. During my grandfather's professional career, he not only discovered the geographical boundary of China's population (瑷珲-腾冲线, Aihuī – Téngchōng line) that also divided the population areas of China, he also formulated a new, different population policy, created a Chinese agricultural division, revealed the population-food relationship and popularized meteorological science. He conducted research on the reduction of the provinces and districts to prevent separatism, facilitated the country's administrative and social life and other outstanding achievements.

My grandfather's most famous scientific achievement was the discovery of the geographical boundary of China's population, also known as the Aihuī – Téngchōng line, which is referred to as the Hu Huanyong line at home and abroad. At that time, my grandfather used the information of the Hukou, the household registration of the National Government, to draw the map of China, using the 20000 people mark to draw a map of China with the population distribution and characteristics. From Aihui in Heilongjiang to Tengchong in Yunnan, an imaginary line dividing China into two parts. The south-eastern part of the Hu Huanyong line has 96% of the population and 36% of the country's land area. The altitude is low, and the rainfall is abundant. The oxygen content of the air is entirely adapted to human life with rapid economic development and high national income. The north-western part of the Hu Huanyong line has a population of only four percent, but the land area is 64%. The high altitude, low rainfall, low air oxygen content is not suitable for large-scale human life. Economic development is slow, consequently the national income is low.

The magic of Hu Huanyong's line is not the explanation at the time of publication. Today, more than 80 years later, in spite of the rapid development of China, not only has the proportion of population in south-eastern and north-western China not changed significantly; also, agriculture, meteorology, geology, urban distribution, ecological environment and scenery remain the same. Places of interest, highways, etc. can all be inspired by the research of the Hu Huanyong line. According to my grandfather's own explanation, the Aihuī – Téngchōng line is a geographically dividing line of population, gradually shaped by history. It is a comprehensive product of nature, economy and history. It is a reflection of objective laws of nature. According to my understanding, the Hu Huanyong line is the dividing line of China's national conditions for studying various social phenomena in China.

In the past few years, tourists and media have visited the Hu Huanyong line. Recently, several media organizations have interviewed me in Nanjing. The working group of the News Network has also visited the Hu Huanyong line. Including the interviews in Nanjing, there have been more than 10 special reports published. China's online media group NetEase News Network also came to Nanjing to see Hu Huanyong's former residence and the Central University campus. They interviewed me. The future of Hu Huanyong's line will be reported to the Chinese society and recognized by a broad audience.

My grandfather's academic career spanned the period of the Republic of China and the People's Republic of China for nearly 70 years with diligent work and writings. Not only is the influence of the Hu Huanyong line well-known in China, but many of his discourses are still recognized by the Chinese government and have important guiding significance for today's Chinese studies.

## 4. Some considerations regarding the National Central University and the Nanjing University

The National Central University [NCU, 中大 Zhōng dà] has a long history. Shortly before the Japanese invasion of China in 1937, the Nanjing massacre and the occupation of Nanjing, NCU moved from Nanjing to Chongqing in south-western China. After the victory of the Anti-Japanese War in 1945, NCU returned to Nanjing's original site.

But then, when the Chinese Communist Party came to power in 1949, NCU was renamed National Nanjing University. Three years later, in 1952, the government changed China's university education system as per the Soviet system. Nanjing University only retains the School of Science and the College of Liberal Arts among the Central University's seven colleges. The NCU School of Engineering became independent as the Nanjing Institute of Technology. The NCU Teachers College became independent as the Nanjing Normal University. The NCU College of Agriculture also became independent as the Nanjing Agricultural College. The NCU Medical School went to Shanghai and Changsha. The School of Business and Law moved to Shanghai to become the Shanghai University of Finance and Economics and the East China Political Science and Law. All these former Nanjing University divisions and colleges are now among the best universities in China.

My grandfather used to be the director of the Department of Geography of the Central University and the director of the research department. In 1943, during the chairmanship of Jiang Zhongzheng, he asked my grandfather to serve as the provost of the Central University and take charge of the Central University's teaching. Although the conditions in all aspects were very difficult during the Anti-Japanese War, the university developed rapidly. Among

the 45 national-level professors hired by the Ministry of Education
of the National Government in 1942, there were 12 in the Central
University and 9 in the Southwestern Associated University. These
professors were the most famous and renowned professors in China.
Southwest Union University was established by Tsinghua University,
Nankai University and Peking University during the special time
of the War of Resistance. At that time, they moved to Kunming in
the south.

After the end of the Anti-Japanese War, Tsinghua University
and other students returned to Beijing and Tianjin. The Central
University also moved back to its former location in Nanjing.

During the Anti-Japanese War, the National [KMT] Government
moved to Chongqing in 1937, so did the National Central
University. In 1940, [after three years of Japanese occupation] Wang
Jingwei established the pro-Japanese traitor government in Nanjing.
He also established the 'Central University' in Nanjing, which
was later called the 'Fake-Zhongda'. The students who studied at
this university were called 'fake-students'. Jiang Zemin, who later
became the head of the Communist Party of China, was a student
at that 'Fake-Central University'. During the Anti-Japanese War,
the students and teachers of the Central University who moved to
Chongqing in the west were all wearing military [KMT] uniforms.
They had a great sense of honour and looked down on the traitor
university that cooperated with the Japanese. After the victory of the
Anti-Japanese War, the 'Pseudo-Central University' disbanded itself,
the National Central University moved back to Nanjing, refusing to
recognize the 'pseudo' Central University students' accomplishments
and diplomas. The students who lost their academic status took to
the streets to express their anger. The government later tolerated
these students by admitting them to other universities to complete

their studies. That's why Jiang Zemin went to Shanghai Jiaotong University to study engineering. After all, this is an embarrassing history. Therefore, Mr. Jiang Zemin himself only admitted being a graduate of Shanghai Jiaotong University and actively participated in the commemoration activities of the National Jiaotong University. He was always embarrassed to admit that he had studied at the (fake) Nanjing University (Central University).

Currently, the specific funding allocation of the Nanjing University is not very clear. In the past, Tsinghua University focused on preparing students for further study in the United States, getting sufficient support from the church.
The Central University however was a national [KMT] university and one of the best universities in China, even in Asia. The National Government is still very concerned about the Central University. After 1949, Tsinghua University was in the Beijing, the new capital, many national leaders were trained here. The funding of Nanjing University was significantly affected.

Today, Chinese universities are controlled by the Communist Party. Tsinghua University is in the capital, and the central government has a great influence. The intellectuals are subject to restrictions. Nanjing University is far away from Beijing and is less affected, but it is still under the direct control of the central government. The university principal and Party secretary are also appointed by the central government. This political system is very weird. Obviously, this so-called double-headed system is backward and inefficient, but it is still stubbornly insisted on by a large number of officials.

I have thoroughly studied the history of the Nanjing University and I can confirm what I have mentioned. It's a pity that we don't have the time today, otherwise I could accompany you to the Nanjing University and the History Museum of the Southeast University.

## 5. Family and work experience

My father was the eldest son of Hu Huanyong. He graduated from the National Central University School of Science in 1947 and worked for the Ministry of Finance of the National Government. After 1949, he was a professor at Nanjing University of Aeronautics and Astronautics and my mother was a professor at Nanjing Medical University.

At the beginning of the Cultural Revolution in 1966, I graduated from elementary school. During the Cultural Revolution, I stopped working for some time. Later, I became an electronics factory worker engaged in mechanical processing. I also worked as a mechanical designer and factory manager and later I was in trade and consulting company services. Because of the political troubles, I didn't have the opportunity to get a formal education.

I mainly learned by self-study and by evening work. I took mechanical engineering and industrial management courses. I managed a company. One day, a supplier gave me a pair of shoes, but I put them under my desk; I never used these shoes. Another one gave me money; I refused. I believe that people at a certain age who have done good things should keep in mind that the bad things they do will be punished.

I am not a member of the Chinese Communist Party. I'm 64 now and retired. I mainly study my grandfather's work, study reports related to my grandfather. I sometimes have media interviews

and I give lectures. I hope to give young people some insights and
assistance in understanding the history of China.

My wife is retired from work at Nanjing Airport. Our daughter
is finishing her Master of Pharmacy at the Pittsburgh School of
Pharmacy University. After graduation she will return to work
in Nanjing.

## 6. My understanding of Chinese society today

China's economy has developed rapidly in recent years. The
advantage of the centralized system is that it can quickly mobilize
and focus economic resources to drive economic take-off and
employment. The economic development since the Cultural
Revolution is indispensable for the expansion of the country's
economic growth and the improvement of our living standard. No
doubt about that.

At the same time, we also see that economic development with
investments as the main feature has promoted the rapid expansion
of production capacity in various industries, but it also has a great
impact on environmental protection, resource utilization, national
education and living standards. There is a serious imbalance in the
development in various areas. The gap between the rich and the poor
in national income is growing, social frictions are growing. The cost
of maintaining government stability is getting higher.

In the past decades, China's political mechanism has not followed
that pace. The appointment and promotion of Chinese officials is
not by election by the people who need these services. It is not the
ability to be suitable for the job, but by appointment by the top. This
political system is characterized by a concentration of power in the

hands of a small number of people who only need to speak, and work as required by the leadership. Not everyone accepts that: people will not speak out; they won't say what they're thinking or what's happening. In their public speeches, Communists sound unison but their true beliefs are different from what they say in public. The so-called firm stance of 'communist beliefs' is just a slogan.

China has a vast number of officials. Their living standards are much better than those of ordinary people. Their children seldom engage in academic careers such as professors or scientists. Many of them live abroad; of those who stay in the country are business leaders, they're in finance or politics at various levels. We have seen many important institutions and officials bending the law; corruption is staggering. Many officials have lived a very comfortable life; they have taken money that didn't belong to them. Some of them are convicted and in prison.

I don't think 'dissidents' in China are terrible. Facing the political problems in China, I have actively considered suggestions for improving the political system. I believe that most of them are patriotic and hoping that the country will gradually improve. If our country would tolerate criticism and listen to different opinions in the society, it would be a huge impetus for China's development and progress. We should rely on the experience of more advanced countries to improve or own political and economic system. In regard to this point, from the end of the Cultural Revolution in 1976 to the political turmoil in 1989, the great role of reform and opening up in promoting social progress is very obvious for every Chinese person.

In the Second World War, Chinese officials claimed that the Japanese army killed 300,000 people in the Nanjing Massacre during the war against China. They built a memorial hall in Nanjing to commemorate these lost lives.

But also after 1949, there were dozens of political movements of all kinds and sizes. Many innocent people have died from all kinds of violence and illicit crimes. For example, the so-called 'repression of counter-revolution' has killed many small landlords and junior officials, many of whom have helped the Communist Party to succeed. After the end of the Cultural Revolution, the government confessed to the persecution of many persecutors of the previous 'movements'.

Today, the Chinese government still hasn't apologized for their attitude during the Cultural Revolution [1976-1989], neither for the one that began in 1966. Some people even wrote that these political movements had a positive effect on China's society. People are not satisfied. And because the government refused to reflect and open the archives, the younger generation knew almost nothing about the tragedy of the society at that time. This is not a scientific, rational approach. We should learn from the German government, admit mistakes and prevent this sin from happening again.

The Chinese are very forgiving. We hope that the Chinese government can correctly explain the sins of history, punish the responsible officials, apologize and compensate the people who have been treated unfairly so that young people can correctly understand this history. Let the families of these victims face the truth and work convincingly to build a better future for China.

China has made rapid progress in all fields; the society has spawned many new occupations. Young people have great competitive pressure, they're not interested in political participation. The same is true for Chinese college students; many young people do not understand history. At my age, I hope that by telling the misfortune of the Chinese experience that I know of, that the society and future generations can understand the truth of history and avoid the recurrence of the past and the turmoil we have experienced.

Over the years, the media interviewed me about my grandfather's life story and the Hu Huanyong line. Before you publish this, I ask you to submit it to me. I am a descendant of a scientist; I can't allow mistakes. As per my experience, many of the published manuscripts have made mistakes. Western countries are different from Chinese culture and easily have misunderstandings about China's development.

**Some basics about the Hu-line (the Heihe–Tengchong line)**

In 1935, Hu Huanyong, my grandfather, concluded his geography and population research with the Heihe - Tengchong line, in the West called the Hu-line.

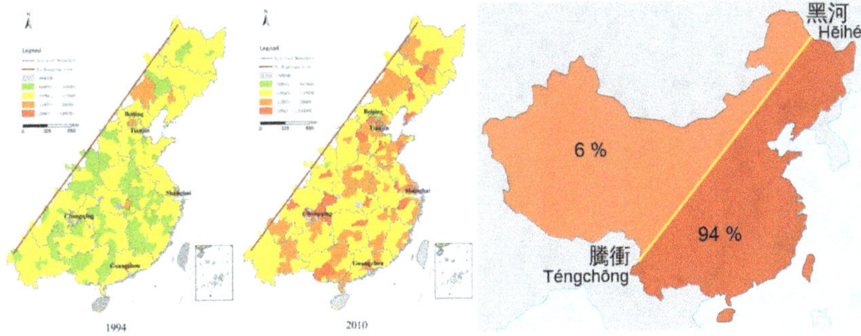

*Fig. 28 Population growth and migration   Fig. 29 The Hu (Heihe–Tengchong) Line
S.E. of the Hu line*

The surface area of China is 9597 million km². Only 15% is economically viable. The two main conditions to be viable are:

1.  Maximum 200 m height
2.  At least 500 mm rainfall per year

There's nothing the Chinese government can do to change these two conditions.
Currently, there is research ongoing to change or move the natural rainfall and there's also research to possibly explode and flatten some uninhabited mountainous regions in Xizang -Tibet. But up to now, that are just very wild ideas.

Shanghai Pudong New Bund Church

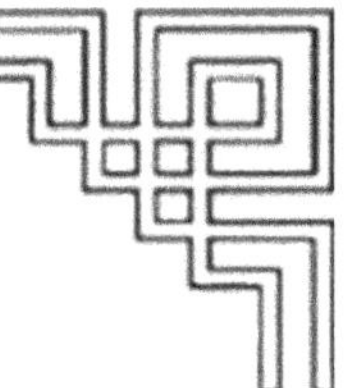



# 22.

# Philanthropy with Chinese Characteristics.

*#philanthropy #benevolence #grassroots–activities
#volunteering #charity*

*Charity has long been a part of the religion, culture and traditions of China. Whilst the concept is not new, new technological and societal innovations have helped revolutionise philanthropy in China. Thanks to social media and the support of the government, charities around China are now more successful and under the spotlight than ever.*

Helping others is encouraged in every culture in the world but even more in China. Charity is important not only because of the way it helps people, but al-so to maintain the aura of sympathy and kindness in the atmosphere of the country. China is very upfront and persistent with the roles of charities in society.

## Philanthropy with Chinese characteristics: a game changer for the world of charity.

Philanthropy in China today is in a state of expansion, experimentation and evolution. Its origins and the charitable motivations of the country's new philanthropists are deeply rooted in traditional Chinese values. Yet at the same time there are new exciting philanthropic initiatives in China, built on high-tech innovations to create new evolutions in philanthropy for mankind.

Between 2010 and 2016, donations from the top 100 philanthropists in mainland China more than tripled to CNY 33 billion[87], while the number of registered foundations in China surged to 5545, a 430% increase over a decade.[88]

---

87  Paula D. Johnson and Tony Saich, "Values and Vision: Perspectives on Philanthropy in 21st Century China.", *Harvard Kennedy School ASH Center*, 20.10.2019
https://www.international.ucla.edu/media/files/GCPI-Tsinghua-Forum-Program-Booklet-vb-uq2.pdf
88  "GCPI – Global Chinese Philanthropy Initiative", *Schwarzman College, Tsinghua University*, 28.06.2018
https://www.international.ucla.edu/media/files/GCPI-Tsinghua-Forum-Program-Booklet-vb-uq2.pdf

The National People's Congress (NPC) in China enacted the Charity Law in 2016, which played a key role in boosting charities.

Philanthropy has a very long history in China – several dynasties were driven by charity and thrive on it – but it has been a relatively new phenomenon for the current younger generation as, since the establishment of the People's Republic of China in 1949, wealth has been nationalized and philanthropy maligned.

In recent decades, philanthropy in China has been surging and slowly developing into a valuable asset for China's future. Charity in China has its own long history and also has its own motivations and considerations today and certainly its own direction and methods for the future. Characteristic Chinese philanthropy is not just a blind copy of Western-style philanthropy.

**History of philanthropy in China**

Philanthropy and charity have been inherent to most civilizations and dynasties throughout China's ancient history.

The relatively modest level of giving in modern-day China is something of an anomaly in China's long history. The notion of charity is deeply embedded in the ethical premises of Confucianism, Buddhism and Daoism, creating a strong moral obligation to help others. These ethical mores were typical up until the secularisation that accompanied the Chinese revolution of 1949. Over many centuries charitable giving in China established firm roots and characteristics which can even be witnessed today in the sense of charity among people in China and Chinese people abroad.

Under the various pre-1911 dynasties and in Republican China

(1911 - 1949), local communities and trading organizations
gave donations through temples or associations to build schools,
orphanages and hospitals; to provide assistance during famine or
natural disasters; and, given the cultural importance of ancestor
veneration and the afterlife, to help families who could not afford the
cost of burial.

In most dynasties, trade, beliefs and governance were closely
linked. Keeping communities well, healthy and respected through
country magistrates' charities implied that they had strong ethical,
moral, financial motivations as well as a strong sense of planning
for prosperity. During the Song dynasty (960-1279), local county
magistrates and powerful merchants provided charity to the destitute
and impoverished, including the operation of poorhouses and
subsidization of burial costs.

During the Ming Dynasty (1368 - 1644), private foundations
('benevolent societies') supported by elites controlling the salt trade
monopoly emerged and were significant sources of philanthropy to
keep communities respected and developed.

The salt trade monopoly in China is the oldest continuous state
monopoly in the world, having been established for more than 2000
years – it was only been partially dismantled during recent years.
The monopoly has existed since before the Han Dynasty (221 - 206
BCE), predating the construction of the Great Wall. In 119 BCE,
Emperor Wu of Han cast about for ways to finance his expansionist
policies, and at the urging of his legal advisors, he decreed salt to be a
state monopoly, and this has remained operational until today.

An important shift in philanthropy occurred in the 19th century
with the arrival of foreign philanthropies in China, initially linked

to the work of missionaries. Much of the work of these foreign philanthropic organizations was linked to introducing foreign health care and religions.

In 1949 with the establishment of the People's Republic of China, all wealth was nationalized, and philanthropy maligned. Any recognition of the need for private charity for schooling or sustenance was seen as a sign of state failure.

However, the deeply rooted sense of collectiveness has survived since 1949 through charity support within families. In the case of strong lineages were strong, charitable estates have long provided for the schooling and health care of poorer members of extended families, which could comprise an entire community. Nevertheless, private philanthropic initiatives and non-governmental organisations (NGOs) were shut down and foreign philanthropists were told to leave China. Philanthropy in China stagnated for the next 30 years.

**Philanthropy in China since the 1980s.**

With the country's economic reforms in the 1980's, China's philanthropic landscape began to revive, admittedly slowly and cautiously at first. The historical philanthropic legacies described formed the foundation for the revival. Building on these traditions, three key factors have contributed to the surging development of today's modern philanthropic sector.

**First,** as described, is the remarkable expansion of private wealth that escalated once China entered the World Trade Organization in 2001. This has led not only to a sharp rise in the number of wealthy, but also to the rapid expansion of the middle class, members of which are exhibiting a significant interest in charitable causes.

While private wealth alone is not a sufficient prerequisite for a
robust philanthropic sector, it is an important ingredient, and
it provides the foundation for a potentially explosive growth in
philanthropy in China.

**A second** critical factor in the development of the modern
philanthropic sector is the Chinese government's shift in attitude
towards philanthropy and the provision of social services. New
social needs created as a result of reforms could not be fulfilled by
the government or the market alone – consequently, alternative
vehicles for the provision of services have become necessary to
supplement the work of government agencies. In addition, the
government wished to turn public service units – such as hospitals,
scientific research organizations and museums – into not-for-profit
organizations, and wanted to open new channels of funding for
them (including the ability to accept public donations) to avoid their
collapse and the attendant unemployment that would result.

**The third** factor in the sector's expansion is the rapid rise of non-
governmental organizations (NGOs). At the start of 2016, there
were 662000 social organizations formally registered with the
Ministry of Civil Affairs, with perhaps another three million
unregistered organizations. Most of these are local organizations
working on issues of health, education or poverty alleviation. Of
those registered, around half are 'social groups' which correspond
most closely to the Western definition of an NGO; almost one half
comprises private non-enterprise units, including public service units.
Approximately 5000 are foundations. This growth has provided
both entities that can receive philanthropic giving. In 2015, non-
governmental organizations received CNY 61.03 billion in donations.

While reported philanthropic contributions are still comparatively low, amounting to only 0.16% of China's 2014 GDP, philanthropy is developing rapidly. China now has a full range of philanthropic mechanisms.

**The 2016 Charity Law:**
On 16th March 2016, the National People's Congress (NPC) voted 2636 to 131 in favour of a new Charity Law in China. The new law was enacted in September 2016, a milestone in providing more legitimacy to the philanthropic sector and encouraging its growth, consistent with government priorities.[89]

Although charity is still perceived with a lot of suspicion by many people due to lack of transparency, it is expected that the new law will be supplemented by clear and transparent guidelines and supporting legislation. With the new law, a much clearer picture is emerging of how the CPC is hoping to encourage the application of at least some of China's new wealth to address social challenges.

**Philanthropy in China today and tomorrow**

Philanthropy in modern-day China is in a state of expansion, experimentation and evolution. Its origins and the charitable motivations of the country's new philanthropists are deeply rooted in traditional Chinese values.

The deep-rooted spirit of volunteering also has an important spiritual dimension, having absorbed the essence of traditional Chinese philanthropic values. What's more, combined with intrinsic advantages, the volunteering spirit gives a new dimension to the philanthropic culture of the present time.

---

89  "China. Charity Law adopted", 17.05.2016
https://www.loc.gov/law/foreign-news/article/china-charity-law-adopted/

Yet at the same time there are new exciting philanthropic initiatives in China, built on high-tech innovations to create new evolutions in philanthropy for mankind.

Philanthropic giving in China is growing rapidly, gaining visibility, and displaying exciting ingenuity and innovation.

**Hurun China Philanthropy List 2018.**[90]

The Hurun China Rich List divulges the names of China wealthiest individuals: in 2018, the list contained information about the top 100 individuals to have made public donations to foundations, NGOs and educational institutions in mainland China. In 2018, 76-year-old He Xiangjian, founder of the Midea Group, was named the most generous philanthropist in China, with CNY 7.5 billion worth of donations. The second and third places were taken by two property (real estate) moguls, 60-year-old Xu Jiaxin, with CNY 3.42 billion worth of donations, and 68-year-old Lu Zhi Qiang with one billion.

The report calculates cash and cash-related donations, as well as promises made with legal force, between 1st April 2018 and 31st March 2019. In accordance with 2017, the donations of the individuals listed account on average for 0.5% of their personal assets. Only 13 women made it to the list, somewhat lower than the female proportion (25.8%) in the Hurun Rich List. The total donations of the 100 philanthropists increased by 33% compared to the previous year, reaching CNY 21.8 billion. To be able to make it onto the list, one had to donate at least 16 million yuan, 6.7% more than the figure for 2017. "The increase in the amount of donations is quite

---

90  "Hurun China Philanthropy List 2019", 21.05.2019
http://www.hurun.net/EN/Article/Details?num=93E8C4B53DE6

obvious. On average they are 10 times as large as the donations that were made 15 years ago, when we compiled the first Philanthropy List," said Rupert Hoogewerf, the Luxembourg-born chief researcher and CEO of Hurun Report.

**Tech-enabled philanthropy in China: the great game-changer.**

New technologies in China have helped to bring innovative approaches to philanthropy and have encouraged broader participation in recent years. Tech giants, in particular, have already learned to take advantage of their branded merchandise to involve the general public in philanthropic activities. For example, in response to the 2008 Wenchuan earthquake in Sichuan, Tencent – the company behind China's biggest social network WeChat/Weixin as well as the largest gaming company in the world – established an online donation platform. More than half a million people contributed, raising a total of CNY 20750000. Tencent added donation options to WeChat, the instant messaging and social media app with one billion monthly active users, and allowed users to give any amount with a swipe of a finger, making philanthropic engagement easier than ever.

New technologies have created more diverse ways of giving. The rising popularity of fitness apps in China has inspired tech companies to incentivize giving among the younger, more health-conscious generation. Through the Xingshan ('doing good') app developed by the Beijing-based company iMore, users record the number of steps they take each day, which is then 'donated' to charities through corporate sponsors. By the end of 2015, users of Xingshan had walked a total of 2.8 million kilometres, raising more than CNY 33000000 for 52 different public welfare organizations and projects.

Facing the troubled reputations of some charitable organizations, new types of charity platforms have stepped in to address both transparency and accountability issues. Real-time updates on donation collections, along with different verification systems, guarantee the funding reaches the right people at the right time. Jian Charity for example – launched by Alibaba's Cainiao Logistics in 2016 – is an online donation platform where people can place orders and then track the real-time location online of the items they donated.

**A new era for philanthropy with differentiated characteristics**

With the deep-rooted sense of collectiveness alongside the expansion of China's private wealth and high-tech innovations, philanthropy in the country is on an undeniably upward trajectory. New technologies are unlocking more inventive forms of giving, which become more synergized with mega-business ecosystems. Public awareness about philanthropy is rising, while non-profit organizations are regaining their credibility and trustworthiness.

In the coming decades, the rise and impact of philanthropy by Chinese people and NGOs in China and abroad will become more and more visible all over the world. It is important to keep in mind that Chinese-style philanthropy is not a blind copy of concepts of philanthropy in the West. It clearly has its own characteristics, motivations and ancient roots. Chinese philanthropic motivations start from ethical foundations; they incorporate personal and corporate responsibilities to give back, and they promote harmonious and respected societies, collective standards and opportunities.

Although it is not as straightforward as this, it is fair to say that one might generally distinguish the motivations of Chinese philanthropy

as having collective, harmonious objectives, while Western
philanthropists might be more characterized by their objectives
towards the individual and diversity.

## Entrepreneurs, celebrities and charitable foundations: elite philanthropy in China. [91]

Foundations provide the basis for philanthropy by the wealthy in
developed countries such as the United States and are playing a
growing role in the development of elite philanthropy in mainland
China. There is no precise definition of the term 'elite philanthropy'
because the words 'elite' and 'philanthropy' imply social and economic
differentiation and hence are essentially contested concepts. Broadly
speaking, elite philanthropy refers to the charitable donations and
activities of particularly wealthy people and thus to philanthropy
by people at the top of an economic hierarchy. These people may
also occupy a position of high social standing as the result of birth,
achievement or good fortune, or they may be viewed as people
who aspire to be seen as social elites and engage in philanthropic
activities to 'buy' respectability and reputation, by deflecting
any 'bad press' associated with their acquisition of private wealth
(Adams 2009 and Ostrower 1995). Whichever the case may be,
'big money philanthropy' is a new phenomenon in the People's
Republic of China.

The groundwork for the establishment of a 'private' philanthropy
sector in the PRC was laid when in 2004 the State Council
issued the Regulations on the Management of Foundations.

---

91   Elaine Jeffreys, "Entrepreneurs, Celebrities and Charitable Foundations: Elite
Philanthropy in China," in *Handbook of Welfare in China*, ed. Beatriz Carrillo Garcia,
Johanna Hood and Paul Cadetz (Cheltenham: Edward Elgar, 2017) Page 1/33
https://www.academia.edu/34347302/Entrepreneurs_Celebrities_and_Charitable_
Foundations_Elite_Philanthropy_in_China

Before then and up until 2010, the PRC's non-profit sector
was dominated by government-organized non-governmental
organizations (GONGOs), especially government-initiated
foundations. An official non-profit sector first emerged in the
PRC in the 1990s following the issuing of the Regulations on
Foundation Management in October 1988 and the Regulations
on the Registration and Management of Social Organizations in
October 1989. [92] However, the regulations stipulated that non-profits
required a government sponsor to be legally registered. This situation
favoured the registration of GONGOs, which were sponsored by the
government agency that established them, while nongovernmental
organizations (NGOs) without the necessary connections found it
difficult to acquire a sponsor. [93]

The 2004 Regulations on the Management of Foundations altered
the shape of China's non-profit sector by permitting the registration
of two different types of foundations:

'public fundraising foundations' (gōngmù jījīn huì 公募基金会),
which can raise funds from the public;

'non-public fundraising foundations' (fēi gōngmù jījīn huì 非公募基
金会), which are not allowed to raise funds publicly and must rely on
private funding from individuals or organizations. [94]
Public fundraising foundations generally refer to GONGOs, while
'non- public fundraising foundations' generally refer to foundations
established with funding from wealthy individuals and private
corporations. A small number of foundations that were founded

---

92  (2011), 'Preface', 'Essential background on the nonprofit, philanthropic sector in
China', and 'Key findings: The good, the bad and the murky', China Development Brief,
2–8.

93  Ibid.

94  Ibid.

with private funds, such as the One Foundation, are permitted to
raise public funds, and some non-public foundations are GONGOs.
[95] In 2004, there were less than 900 public foundations and no non-
public domestic foundations registered in the PRC. [96] In 2010, the
1098 non-public foundations in the PRC surpassed the number of
1077 public foundations for the first time.[97] By mid-2014, there were
nearly 4000 foundations in the PRC, comprising around 2500 non-
public foundations and 1500 public foundations. Although these
figures are tiny when compared to the 86000 private foundations
registered in the US in 2013,[98] the fact remains that there are now
more non-public than public foundations in the PRC.

The rise of privately-funded foundations in mainland China may
be interpreted in different ways. For the Ministry of Civil Affairs
of the PRC, the growth of non-public foundations is an evolving
success story and an important new force for social cohesion and
development. It demonstrates the effectiveness of new policy
frameworks to promote a philanthropic culture in China and the
willingness of wealthy individuals to support government efforts to
enhance social welfare provision. For practitioners of philanthropy,
the growth of non-public foundations has the potential to encourage
more diverse forms of philanthropy. It could provide an alternative
source of funding for NGOs, encourage a focus on neglected areas
or issues other than those backed by government, and improve
professional standards and financial transparency. [99]. For critics,
the growth of privately-funded foundations in China, as in other
parts of the world, is problematic because for them, philanthropy
is 'no substitute for strong governmental support for social

---

95  Ibid.
96  Ibid.
97  Ibid.
98  Ibid.
99  Ibid.

welfare'.[100] The global rise of business-style philanthropies founded
by extraordinarily wealthy individuals, or 'philanthro-capitalism'
to use the term popularized by economists Matthew Bishop and
Michael Green (2008), is criticized for making social welfare the
responsibility of 'unaccountable' business elites and celebrities, and
for legitimizing wealth concentration (and hence inequality) by
suggesting that 'the rich can save the world'.[101] These competing
interpretations turn on different understandings of what constitutes
appropriate social welfare policy. 'Social welfare policy' refers to the
principles, activities or framework for action adopted by national
governments, and advocated by international organizations, to ensure
socially defined levels of individual, family, community, national and
global wellbeing.[102] Such policy is often characterized in terms of an
opposition between 'welfare states' and 'neoliberal states'.

Welfare states, whether liberal-democratic or socialist, traditionally
attempted to protect the health and wellbeing of their citizens,
especially those in need, by subsidizing housing, healthcare and
education, and providing retirement, disability, unemployment
and maternity pensions. In contrast, the role of government in
contemporary neoliberal states is arguably limited to safeguarding
the free market and providing only a minimum level of security
against poverty. Although critics of the welfare state ideal
maintain that it is inefficient, bureaucratic and encourages 'welfare
dependency', supporters criticize neoliberal states for privatising
and individualising welfare provision through fee-paying services,
and insurance and superannuation schemes, which are not equally
accessible to all.[103] Thus, the PRC's post-1978 abandonment
of socialist-style centralized planning and partial adoption of

---

100  Ibid.
101  Ibid.
102  Ibid.
103  Ibid.

market-based economic reforms is praised for lifting more than 860 million of people out of absolute poverty,[104] but criticized for generating income inequalities and obviating any perceived or actual commitment on the part of the PRC government to providing comprehensive social welfare.[105]

China's newly rich have been encouraged to participate in and create a culture of elite philanthropy, without reducing explanations to idealized notions of how social welfare services and philanthropy should be organised institutionally. A small group of non-public foundations established by some of the most 'rich' and 'famous' people in China, of which the founders have close interactions with government, elite politics and the media. The objective of analysing this sample is to obtain a 'snapshot' of how elite-funded charitable foundations currently operate. Standard western critiques of 'philanthro-capitalism' provide an incomplete account of the political economy of elite philanthropy in China. The government is neither simply outsourcing welfare provision to 'unaccountable' business-celebrity elites and nor do privately-funded foundations in the main work independently entirely fill all gaps in the government's provision of public services.

Elite philanthropists in China typically operate hand in glove with the government on 'core' welfare and humanitarian initiatives while mobilizing more limited financial resources and their elite political connections to pursue peripheral independent interests.

Philanthropy with Chinese characteristics: it might be a game-changer for philanthropy in the future global society.

---

104 Ibid.
105 Ibid.

Beijing Haidian Christian Church

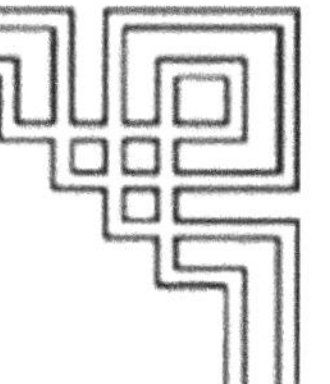

# Christianity in China.

*#Christianity #Catholicism #Protestantism #SARA #UFWD*

*Despite difficulties and challenges regarding gathering religious data, it is evident that Christianity has been on a very uphill rise in the last few years. Going from only 3 million a few decades ago to roughly 100 million devotees today is a staggering rise. These Christians identify with subsidiaries such as Catholic, Protestant and even other groupings of Christianity.*

Religious demographics are one of the most important data that the government must have about the population of the country. This is so that the needs and wants of the people can be met. Furthermore, the government is ensuring that the environment of the country is welcoming to diverse religions and mindsets.

Christianity in China is rapidly growing, although in the past three years the growth has not been as fast as in the past three decades. Christianity is by large the fastest-growing religion in China, rising from just three million adherents four decades ago to as many as an estimated 100 million today. Exact figures about the number of Christians are difficult to obtain. What follows is an attempt to create some clarity in the chaos of the various estimations of the number of Christian groups in China.

Until 2018, the State Administration for Religious Affairs (SARA) was a department under the State Council (constitutionally synonymous with the Central People's Government) to manage religious affairs in China. Today, SARA no longer exists; religious issues are now managed directly by the UFWD (United Front Work Department).

The data for this essay was compiled in consultation with:
- Fr. Jeroom Heyndrickx, founder and president of the Ferdinand

Verbiest Foundation and member of the Vatican Commission
on China [106]

- Ian Johnson, author of *The Souls of China: The Return of Religion After Mao* [107]
- About a dozen of various other sources, including personal contacts, Christians and others.


**Basic data about the number of Christians in China:**


<u>1 Protestants</u>
There are about 25 million government-registered *patriotic*
Protestants, that's a combination of the Three-Self Patriotic
Movement and the China Christian Council.


There are also same number, twenty-five million *unregistered*
Protestants, the so called 'house' churches, the ex- 'underground'
Protestants.
The term 'unregistered' is preferable instead of 'underground' because
the bulk of them no longer operate in hiding. These days, they're
quite open and the Public Security Bureau knows of their existence.
They're not 'house' churches either because most don't meet in living
rooms anymore. Some few are underground and some do meet in
houses, therefore the term 'unregistered' is more neutral.


<u>2 Catholics</u>
There are about 5 million SARA -registered Catholics in China.
The same amount; about 5 million are unregistered, aka
'underground', 'house' Roman Catholics. They report to Rome.

<hr>

106 Jeroom Heyndrickx, "Historiography of the Chinese Catholic Church. 19th and 20th
Centuries", *Leuven: Ferdinand Verbiest Foundation, 1994, 510pp.*, ISBN 90-801833-2-6.
107  Ian Johnson, "The Souls of China: The Return of Religion After Mao"
*Pantheon, New York, USA, 2017. pp. 480*
https://books.google.be/books?id=vQ6wDAAAQBAJ

<u>3 Others</u>
There is a rapidly rising number of Christians, who do not want to identify with either Protestants or Catholics, and consequently are not registered at the SARA/UFWD. They're sometimes called the 'New Wave' or 'Third Church' [108]

In addition, there are the nondenominational Christians. These are the 'churches' with the self-appointed 'priests'. Their beliefs are often weird, still based on Christianity, but with a mixture of other beliefs. It is as a result of these 'Christians', that Open Doors publish their yearly World Watch List.[109]

In China there are a negligible number of:

- Orthodox Christians (estimation: between 5000 and 20000)
- Jehovah's Witnesses (few but growing)
- Latter Day Saints (Mormons)
- Moonies (Unification movement/-church)

There are almost no Falun Gong or Scientology followers in China. The two are quite similar, yet we can't count them as Christian beliefs.

All this is very rough because there is no reliable survey data, but it's in line with:

- the Pew study showing 60 million Christians
- the *Holy Study Spirit Center* in Hong Kong which reported

---

108  "'Third Church' Movement Emerging in China. Urban Christians make up New Wave" https://virtueonline.org/third-church-movement-emerging-china-urban-christians-make-new-wave
109  Andrew van der Bijl, "Open Doors – World Watch List", 20.10.2019 https://www.opendoors.org

about 10 million Catholics in total, both SARA registered
and unregistered.

- government figures for registered Protestants and Catholics.
- *China Heute*, the German magazine and their regular updates
  on religious statistics.
- confirmation by many Christians that both the registered and
  unregistered churches are about the same size.
- anecdotal observations by several people in China.

The figure of 60 million Christians doesn't match with the 100
million Christians, often mentioned in Western media. Perhaps
the 100 million is based on straight-line extrapolations and not
supported by other survey work.

## In summary, we get to the following table: [110]

| | million | | % |
|---|---|---|---|
| Protestant Three-Self Patriotic Movement | 14 | 24 | 23,3% |
| Protestant China Christian Council | 10 | | 16,7% |
| Protestant "house" churches | 15 | | 25,0% |
| Third Church | 6 | | 10,0% |
| Nondenominational Christianity | 3 | | 5,0% |
| Catholic, Rome | 5 | 12 | 8,3% |
| Catholic, SARA/UFWD | 7 | | 11,7% |
| | 60 | | 100,0% |

| | million | % |
|---|---|---|
| SARA, now UFWD approved | 31 | 51,7 |
| unregistered | 29 | 48,3 |
| | 60 | 100,0 |

Fig. 30 Christianity in China, estimated number of members.

---

110  Christianity in China, estimated numbers. 方腾波 Frans Vandenbosch

**From the table, we derive the following pie chart:** [111]

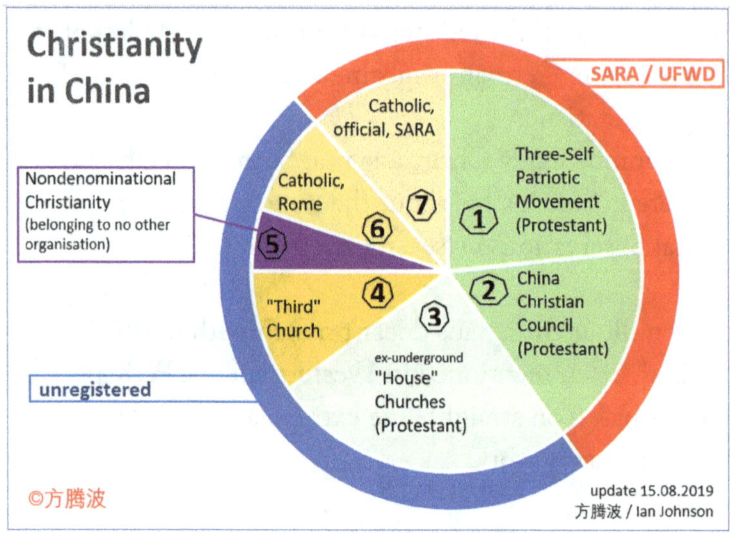


*Fig. 31 Christianity in China, pie diagram ©方腾波*

Obviously, apart from Christianity, there are dozens of other registered and unregistered western and eastern religions, life philosophies, ancestor worshipping and cultural habits in China.

---

111   Christianity in China, pie diagram. 方腾波 Frans Vandenbosch

Shitang Village Internet Conference Center

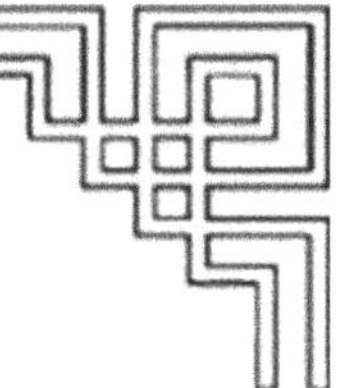



# Focus on the Countryside Villages.

*#teacher #cooperation–leader #village #grassroots*

*Villagers around China have started to take the revitalisation of the countryside into their own hands by building cooperatives and training programs for local residents. The focus is on enhancing the quality of life of rural women and the elderly through recreational and educational workshops. They would also provide rural residents to help with financing and other welfare services. Villagers taking an active role in the provision of social work raised collective awareness of the issues facing rural communities.*

This chapter about Zheng Bing's story is important because it is informative of the village life in China. Whilst the public spotlight is on big cities such as Beijing, the truth is that much of China is made of rural areas and villages. The quality of life in these villages specially in terms of financially happens to be an important factor for the government at all times.

**After an early round of co-ops failed, one village in northern China tried again with a new approach.**

After decades of fast-paced urbanization, China is finally switching gears and starting to address the now-yawning socio-economic divide separating its cities and countryside. Over the past few years, the government has spent huge sums of money in an attempt to raise farmer incomes, alleviate poverty, and "revitalize" the countryside. But the work isn't all state-run: Villagers can and often do take an active part in revitalizing their homes — sometimes in tandem with government initiatives and sometimes on their own.

For much of the 1980s and '90s, I worked as an elementary school teacher in my husband's hometown. Zhaizi Village, which is located along the Yellow River at the junction of Shanxi, Shaanxi, and Henan provinces in north-central China, is in many respects an ordinary Chinese village. When I had free time, I helped my husband run his agricultural supplies store. This gave me plenty of opportunities to interact with other villagers, and I quickly realized that many of them lacked the technical knowledge to know which fertilizers paired best with which crops. In an effort to help, in 1998 I organized a free agricultural training course for local residents.

Zheng Bing explains why she founded a cooperative federation in rural Shanxi, and how it's helped the famers to build a better community.

I soon began trying my hand at other training programs and social organizations, and in 1999, I quit my teaching job to devote myself to this work full time. In 2005, the villagers and I formed our first cooperatives. Almost all of them failed within two years, but in 2012 we tried again, this time with more success. Today, the Puhan Planting Professional Cooperative Federation includes over 3,800 families from three villages and two townships — Puzhou and Hanyang, or Puhan for short.

Back when I was just getting started, one of the first issues I sought to address was the lack of support networks for rural women. During the agricultural off-season, these women generally had little to do other than play mahjong or chat about family matters. Meanwhile, many struggled to break toxic relationship patterns with parents, in-laws, or abusive husbands.

As a rural woman myself, I used to wonder: Why can't our lives be more like those of urban women? I decided to start by organizing a fitness dance class. There was resistance at first: Square dancing had not yet reached the countryside in the early '00s, and many women told me they "wouldn't dare" or that they couldn't dance. But this was mostly because they lacked confidence, and I still believed the activity could help change their mindsets and lifestyles.

I got a teacher to come from the local branch of the All-China Women's Federation, and within a month we went from 24 women dancing in my home's courtyard to roughly 80% of all women in the village. Even the men eventually saw the value in what we were doing. Whereas they would once point fingers at the crazy women dancing, some of the husbands later told me they thought it was good for their wives to dance with "Sister Bing" (me) — in part because it put them in a better mood around the house.

Just improving women's moods wasn't enough, however. Members of our dance group wanted to improve themselves in other ways, too. So in 2001, we decided to organize a study class.

*Fig. 32 Elderly women participate in a calligraphy class in Zhaizi Village, Yongji, Shanxi province, May 30, 2019. Wu Huiyuan*

I found out that 28 of the women in the village had graduated from middle school. I approached them one by one and encouraged them to become team leaders. Next, I organized study groups of three to five people and arranged a joint class for an upcoming Saturday. More than 50 people came that day, including all 28 team leaders.

That year, there just so happened to be a debate competition between college students on television. The study groups decided to hold their own debates, choosing issues from their everyday lives as subjects. Their debate questions included things like: "Who is responsible for maintaining relations between mothers-in-law and daughters-in-law?" and "Is it better to have a son or a daughter?" Everyone took part, and the debate helped village women learn to speak in turn and respect the rules.

Our organization took its next step forward in 2005, when we got in touch with Wen Tiejun, an influential expert on rural China who formulated the sannong, or "three rural issues" of agriculture, development, and farmers. Wen trained us in how to set up rural cooperatives, and we soon formed seven, including a handicrafts co-op and a paint factory. We also built a 160-acre ecological park.

Not everything went smoothly from the start, however. For example, we had 12 households involved in the village's steamed bread workshop. Whenever the bread came out undercooked, everyone blamed someone else. Finding markets was another consistent challenge. Within a few years, most of the co-ops — including the above-mentioned bread workshop, handicrafts co-op, and factory — had failed.

It was clear we lacked management expertise. To resolve this, we had to rethink our mission. In addition to recruiting talented young people to help improve operations, we needed to clarify our goals. That's when we came up with the slogan, "quality of life first, economic growth second." By 2012, when we launched the Cooperative Federation, we had a firmer idea of how to run a cooperative for the good of the village.

*Fig. 33 Villagers relax near the bank of the Yellow River in Zhaizi Village, Yongji, Shanxi province, June 2, 2019. Wu Huiyuan*

*Fig. 34 Children and their parents celebrate Children's Day in Zhaizi Village, Yongji, Shanxi province, June 1, 2019. Wu Huiyuan*

*Fig. 35 A screen-wall featuring the Chinese character 福 fú (blessing, good fortune) in Zhaizi Village, Yongji, Shanxi province, June 2, 2019. Wu Huiyuan*

It wasn't that we didn't want to make money; we just stopped focusing on questions like, "What can we do to make money?" and started asking "How is our money made?" In other words, we didn't want to make money if the cost was too high. If the only way to make a profit spinning yarn was to ask elderly residents to work overtime, we'd rather try something else. We've preferred setting up small, pleasant workshops instead of large factories, and we've opened them to kids from the cities as well as local schools so they can learn more about the production process.

The local government was, and sometimes still is, unsure of what to make of us, since it might seem like we've been doing their job. To us, however, we have just been helping out with something that is near and dear to us: our own village. I've interacted with countless exhausted grassroots public officials over the years, and in that time have come to believe that social organizations should take a much larger role in providing public services. The government should focus on formulating policies and regulations, rather than trying to do everything itself.

There are also important differences between how we do things and how the government does them. Whereas officials tend to prefer providing direct support, we think mutual aid schemes are better at ensuring village buy-in. For example, the state might build an elder care facility for old and retired villagers. This isn't necessarily wrong, but it can inadvertently detach the elderly from their familial care units, as children come to expect the state to take responsibility for their parents' care.

By expecting villagers to take on a more active role in elder care and the provision of other social services, these ties are maintained and reinforced. It also lets us raise collective awareness of the issue. Meanwhile the mutual aid scheme still ensures we can meet baseline needs. The most important thing is getting members of the cooperative to take responsibility for issues that affect their community.

That's because the key to revitalizing China's countryside ultimately lies with its people. Rural residents should be empowered to take the initiative in improving their own lives. Otherwise, revitalizing the countryside will be a long road indeed.

**There is no conflict between economic development and liberty. The development of the countryside was only possible after the national policy became more flexible toward peasants.**

Ye Wende, party secretary in Lin village (near to Xiamen) to Huang Shumin, anthropologist who lived in Iowa, USA before: [112]

"I don't know anything about India or Africa, nor do I know where you have picked up this great idea about the conflict between economic development and liberty. The only thing I know is based on my personal experience, and it seems to run counter to what you said. The more political controls imposed on the peasants, the less they want to work. On the other hand, when the national government shed itself of most controls in the countryside and gave peasants more free choice, they responded with greater enthusiasm and higher production.

This may not be true for all of China. But in Lin village, at least as far as I can tell, it was only in the 1970s, when people realized the absurdity of political campaigns in the countryside and stopped cutting each other's throats, and when the national policy became more flexible toward peasants, that we were able to achieve genuine development. If you don't realize this point, you will never be able to understand current agrarian reform, either at the national level or in this village."

Many westerners may look at China and feel like it is a very controlled country with not much liberty to speak of. Whilst it is widely understood that the living quality in China is far superior to places such as the middle east or Africa, individual freedom is still in question. So far, the Western point of view.

112   Huang Shumin, "The Spiral Road: Change In A Chinese Village Through The Eyes Of A Communist Party Leader" Westview Press, 1989. Published online by Cambridge University Press: 23.03.2011
https://www.cambridge.org/core/journals/journal-of-asian-studies/article/abs/spiral-road-change-in-a-chinese-village-through-the-eyes-of-a-communist-party-leader-by-shumin-huang-boulder-san-francisco-and-london-westview-press-1989-xiv-222-pp-3500-cloth-1595-paper/0200BB50AF28977EAD5D505F238E9DBF#

Contrary to the common western viewpoints, many Chinese villagers that make up the grass root and foundation of the country have very different believes when it comes to individual rights. Examples such as Huang Shumin's book shine light on how the Chinese citizens truly feel. The reality is that there is always a trade-off between collective unity and individual freedom. If individuals are set out to do whatever they please and think incoherently with society, this results in a country like America where everyone is divided on everything. The Chinese government only protects the society from these incoherencies. One can think of this being the government's way of restricting candy and promoting a good brain diet for all individuals. Furthermore, some of the government's ways of control are not always obvious and clear to the conscious mind. For example, one could argue that the fake and biased media in the west is brain washing individuals to have certain presuppositions and biases. This tactic is not often seen as control, but it has a strong foothold on not only what citizens think but also how they think. Villagers in China seem very pleased with the way the country is advancing and growing day to day. China's living conditions are improving faster than ever due to its expanding economy. Many people that left China and came back cannot fathom how much the country has improved since their last visit. The societal coherence, unity and collectiveness that is felt in China is the key to truly getting things done, locally and country wide.

Ningbo New Library

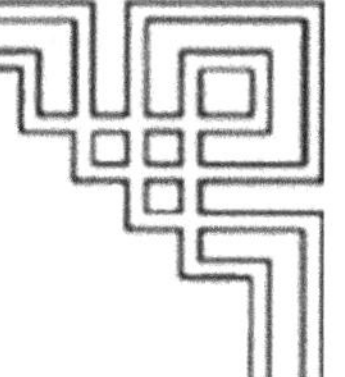

# Baojia, Work Units, Grid Management.

#Baojia #danwei #grid management #work unit

*Modern grid management has increased the efficiency at which events are solved. Modern technology has eased the inspection and division of jurisdictions according to certain standards. The usefulness of this system has been proven by similarities in the American neighbourhood associations and the Buurt Information Netwerk in Holland. This has made it a popular management option around the world and in China.*

Building infrastructure in populous areas such as China can be a daunting task. It is absolutely needed for the government to have a comprehensive plan when it comes to city grids and maps. In China, the new grid management techniques are paving the way for innovation and technology where it is needed most.

## 单位 Dān wèi, 保甲 Bǎojiǎ, 网格化管理 grid management

In China, over the course of history, at least five different grassroots community associations have emerged, all with deep backgrounds in Chinese culture:

**We have to distinct the following similar organisations and systems:**

1. 保甲 bǎojiǎ, (dating back to the Song dynasty, up to 1950, now defunct)
2. 人民公社 rénmín gōngshè (1958 - 1983, now defunct)
3. 单位 dānwèi ('work unit' 1950 - 2003, now defunct)
4. 维稳 wéiwěn ('preserve stability' from 2000 to 2012)
5. 网格化管理 (bad translation: 'grid management system') First trials in 2004 in Dongcheng. Not (yet) in place everywhere in China.

The **American neighbourhood associations** [113] have quite
some similarities with the Chinese grid management system. A
neighbourhood association is a group of neighbours and business
owners who work together for changes and improvements such
as neighbourhood safety, beautification and social activities.
Neighbourhood associations are very distinct from homeowners'
associations which are usually more focused on security issues.

The **BIN (Buurt Information Netwerk) in Flanders and Holland** is
somewhat comparable with the Chinese dānwèi, while the **Hoplr's**[114]
have similarities to Chinese grid management.

According to certain standards, today's modern grid management
relies on unified urban management and digital platforms to divide
urban management jurisdictions into unit grids. By strengthening
the inspection of the cell grid's components and events, separation of
supervision and disposal is established.

Mr. Zhong is a 'grid manager' operating in part of Huayan Beili Xi
Community, a middle-class residential area near Beijing's iconic
bird's nest Olympic stadium. The local government has recruited him
to watch over a 'grid' of streets in the neighbourhood, solve problems
if possible and pass bigger ones up the chain of command for higher-
level attention. The grid system was first pioneered in Dongcheng,
a district of Beijing, in 2004. By 2017 about 60% of China's cities
were using it in some districts according to Zhou Wang of Nankai
University in Tianjin, up from 45% in 2015.

---

113  "Neighbourhood associations", Wikipedia, The Free Encyclopedia, 20.10.2019
Neighbourhood associations - Wikipedia
114  "Hoplr", Wikipedia, The Free Encyclopedia, 20.10.2019
https://nl.wikipedia.org/wiki/Hoplr

*Fig. 36 A 'blue vest' grid manager at work: (source 'smart bixi')*

Tianjin Nankai University former Library

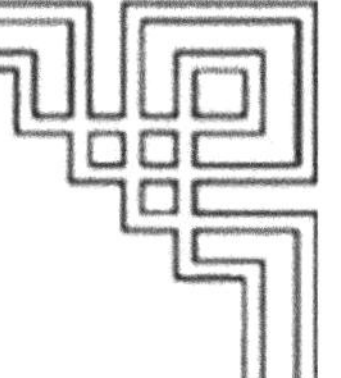



# 26.

# Grid Management Is Not to Maintain Stability.

*#grid #management #wéiwěn #society #stability #harmony*

*Xi Jinping brought with him, along with a new governing style, a different meaning to the Chinese Dream under the influence of the Communist Party. He focuses on maintaining stability in terms of unity amongst the Chinese people. Xi's approach to stability is to facilitate agency through grid management, therefore supporting social cohesion in the long term. This is in contrast with his predecessor, Hu Jintao, who emphasised the Harmonious society but was known for stagnant stability.*

Whilst the communist party retains its ideals and traditions, leaders such as Xi Jinping have brought new influence to this party. It is essential to implement these new ideas because the world, particulary China, is changing at a rapid pace. This section of the book outlines the ways Xi's ideas differ from previous Chinese leaders.

**Before 网格化管理 grid management, there was 维稳 wéiwěn.**

Wéiwěn 维稳 is a verb phrase, not a noun. 维 is a verb meaning 'to maintain' or 'to preserve', with '稳' meaning 'stable' or 'stability', the latter in this case. The full name is apparently 维护国家局势和社会的整体稳定. 'maintaining the overall stability of the nation and society', but 维稳, 'maintaining stability', is an intuitive abbreviation to anybody familiar with the Chinese government.

Xi Jinping seems to still use the phrase 习近平：”维权是维稳的基础 维稳的实质是维权 – 新闻 – 国际在线” but it is not one of his key catchphrases or key political campaign focus points according to SupChina. [115]

---

115 "The 25 Key Phrases of Xi Jinping", *SupChina*, 20.10.2019
https://supchina.com/2016/11/14/25-key-phrases-xi-jinping/

## The Chinese Dream.

Xi Jinping, contrary to his predecessor Hu Jintao, is focussing much more on anti-corruption, moving China up the supply chain, trying to escape the middle-income trap, expanding Chinese business abroad through the Belt and Road Initiative and similar programs, and ensuring that Chinese identity remains decidedly socialist in its prosperity. Basically, the '**Chinese Dream**', but as defined by the Communist Party. He'll make occasional statements that suggest the importance of maintaining social stability, but I think he measures stability as a metric and an effect of other policies, rather than a goal to be pursued in its own right, and I think he's correct. If you get the macro-economy right, if you're winning international prestige and get to avoid culpability for problems, if you can avoid directly speaking about anything negative, then you have political stability. Explicitly talking about crushing your opponents (Duterte or Trump-style) doesn't make them go away, it just focuses attention on them, and if you aren't thoroughly defeating them, this publicity can boost their strength.

Xi also doesn't have to talk about these issues all that much because China is a fundamentally pretty stable place right now. The actual stability is not stable, if that makes sense: it could potentially unravel if there was some big screw-up. The West is a mess right now. The Western bias about Huawei, Tibet, Hong Kong and Uighur issues have only served to unite the Chinese people behind the government. The very few remaining dissidents, most of them sponsored by the NED (National Endowment for Democracy), have largely been discredited. The new law on NGOs and Charity organizations [116]

---

116 "The New Law on Charity and NGOs", 20.10.2019
https://www.loc.gov/law/foreign-news/article/china-charity-law-adopted/

, quite similar to the US FARA [117] (Foreign Agents Registration Act) has made it illegal for foreign intelligence agencies to use NGOs as a cover. Consequently, most of them moved to Hong Kong and Taiwan. This has greatly contributed to the stability of Chinese society.

In the early Xi era, 2013 to 2015, there was some criticism on the concept of 维稳 wéiwěn ('maintain stability'), actually criticism on Hu Jintao. His legacy is seen as one of stability but stagnation. Was Hu Jintao a failure? Not at all. But Xi Jinping, his successor, has another approach: he sees the best defence as a good offense and mostly takes a flanking rather than a direct approach to political opposition such as through his charm offensive to Donald Trump during his visit, or his subtle dropping of all public mention of the Made in China 2025 initiative while also pursuing it wholeheartedly. Beijing's 'Made in China 2025' plan isn't dead, it was out of control. That's Xi Jinping's approach.

Today in China people no longer talk about 维稳 wéiwěn. It was a popular word during the Hu Jintao era, but it is not popular today.

网格化管理 **"Grid management"** (a bad translation) was first introduced under Xi Jinping as something similar to 维稳 wéiwěn, but today, they are very different.

Grid management is more like a facilitating agency. If one villager is coming down with an illness, someone in the grid will inform the grid manager, so the patient will get treatment. Currently, the cities and districts who implement grid management, do so to support

---

117 The Foreign Agents Registration Act, 22 U.S.C. § 611 et seq. (FARA) https://www.justice.gov/nsd-fara

social cohesion, not as a way to maintain stability. Hu Jintao's 维稳 wéiwěn is over.

Hu Jintao used to mention 和谐社会 héxié shèhuì (the Harmonious Society) in almost every speech. But that's something very different from 维稳 wéiwěn. The 和谐 héxié is an old Confucianist notion which is deeply rooted in Chinese society and history.

Chinese politics is efficient; it has the focus on the long term which is inherent to the Chinese meritocracy. Western politics is 'noisier' with a focus on the short term, usually the next elections.

Huateng Hog House Rural Library

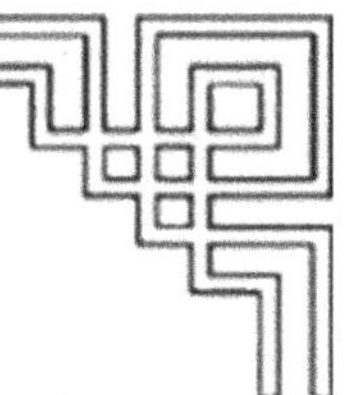

Chapter

# 27.

# Innovations in Social Management.

*#grid #management #meritocracy #society #stability #harmony*
*#wănggé-huà-guănlĭ*

*The Chinese government's organisation is modernising from a traditional plan-economy to a socialist market economy to match current realities and avoid social contradictions. The following structures need to be changed for social management systems to begin continuous development of the socialist market economy: the hierarchy, the urban and rural region, income distribution and the population and family structures. This requires four key aspects to be solved and a more modern social management system to be built. Public resource allocation, including taxation and charity, must be a priority to guarantee social management. To achieve this, human resources for professional social management are to be cultivated and maintained.*

Socialism is taking root in China. When economic systems seek change, lots of other facets of society also must be altered. It is important to understand the change taking place and how it will affect people because if not prepared for, change can be a dangerous event for people.

## The urgent need for innovation and reform in Social Management.[118]

At present, China is in a transition period, moving from a traditional to a modern society, from an agricultural society to an industrial society, from a traditional planned economy to a socialist market economy. The social structure, organization and value concepts have all undergone profound changes. In China, the basic power is highly concentrated, and the government's organisation of all social management methods can no longer meet the new realities. This is the main reason why a large number of social contradictions are prone to occur frequently. Therefore, China has to develop a social

---

118 Lǐ Péilín 李培林, "The urgent need for innovation and reform in Social Management", CPC News Weekly, 20.10.2019.
http://theory.people.com.cn/GB/133473/13990886.html

management theory with Chinese characteristics, innovate the social management system and construct a new social management pattern that is compatible with the development of the socialist market economy. China should achieve social harmony and stability, not just for the obvious glory of academics but to care for the people. It is a major and real problem.

**Social Management** usually refers to government-led and other social management entities. It includes organizing, coordinating, serving, and supervising all aspects of the social field in various ways within the framework of laws, regulations and policies, plus the enforcement process. Since the reform and opening up of China, profound changes have taken place in all areas of the economy and society. The basic power is highly concentrated. The government's overall management of social management has also undergone great changes. However, the existing social management system is still difficult to adapt to the needs of rapid and profound social changes. This requires rethinking the social management laws in depth, updating the concept of social management, integrating social management resources, -systems and -mechanisms and building a new social management pattern.

**The profound changes in the economy and society** since China's reform and opening-up require innovative social management systems.

A prominent feature of the current economic and social situation is the sustained and rapid economic development, the overall political stability and the emergence of social problems. There are many factors causing social problems. One of the important factors is that the existing social management system is difficult to adapt to the rapid and profound changes in the economic society. This urgently requires an innovative social management system.

The profound changes in the social structure require innovative social management systems. With the deepening of reform and opening up and the continuous development of the socialist market economy, China's social and economic components, organizational forms, employment methods, interest patterns and distribution methods are increasingly diversified, and the existing social management system faces some major changes.

**The first is the change in the structure of the hierarchy.** The simple hierarchical structure of the working class, the peasant class, the cadres, traders and academics, which has a small differentiation of interests, has been transformed into a complex hierarchical structure composed of many different interest groups. The remaining farmers are agricultural managers now. The average schooling duration among the Chinese population has risen to 11 years. How to integrate and coordinate the interests of all walks of life in this new situation, forming an order that is both energetic and harmonious becomes an important task of social management.

**The second is the change in urban and rural structure.** More than 200 million rural peasants have left their land and their villages and have turned into workers in the secondary and tertiary industries. The new generation of migrant workers are more eager to live a life different from their parents. How to ensure that these former farmers integrate in their new life in the city becomes a major becomes a major challenge in social management.

**The third is the change in the structure of income distribution.** The Gini coefficient, measuring the degree of equalization of income distribution, has gradually increased. The income gap between urban and rural, regional and social members is widening. Some unfair distribution has caused dissatisfaction among the people. How to adjust the income distribution structure, reverse the income gap expansion trend and establish a fair and reasonable income distribution order is becoming a serious problem, urgently needing to be solved to maintain social harmony and stability.

**The fourth is the change in population and family structure.** In the past few thousand years, the intergenerational pyramid structure in China has begun to appear as an inverted pyramid family structure in the cities. Increasing social mobility and the adjustment of intergenerational relationships have led to the miniaturization of urban and rural households and the reduction of resident family members. The trend is obvious. Many problems that can be solved by family – intergenerational issues such as pensions, single parental care and disease care – have gradually become social problems.

**These are all new social management tasks that China is facing.**

The profound changes of social organization require innovative social management systems. With the profound changes in the economic system, the method of social organization has undergone tremendous changes. This change can be summarized as a change from 'unit person' to 'social person'. On the one hand, with the advancement of reforms such as ownership, employment marketization, social security socialization and logistics service marketization, the 'unit organization', which is the basis of the traditional management system, weakens the ability to solve social problems at grassroots level. Currently, some unit organizations are completely disintegrated. On the other hand – on a positive note – the diversification of employment methods has accelerated social mobility.

Since the reform and opening up of China, many newly created employment-organizations have adopted a 'non-unit' management system. **Among the employed urban population, the membership of work units has fallen from over 95% in the past to about 25% now.** Between the government and the scattered 'social people', the original unit management network is weakening; the new community management network is not optimal, leading to a lack of social integration. Because of that, the government often must face the scattered individuals directly, which increases the cost of governance. The implementation of top-down social affairs and the resolution of bottom-up social issues is hindered. At the same time, some social disputes and grassroots social contradictions cannot be resolved at the grassroots level, leading to an increase in petitions. In some places, social problems have accumulated – grievances due to years of dissatisfaction. This is the main cause of the sudden burst in mass demonstrations and incidents. Therefore, strengthening and improving social management requires new explorations and a new direction of social management, compatible with socialist democracy and market economy.

**Goals, the direction of reform and innovation in social management system:**

Modern social management is an interactive process led by government intervention and coordination, based on grassroots community autonomy and non-profit social organizations as an intermediary to mobilize the public to participate. **From a macro perspective, this requires solving the following three aspects:**

**The first step should be to scientifically understand** the main objectives of the modern social management system. For the first time, the Fourth Plenary Session of the 16th CPC Central Committee proposed to establish and improve the social management pattern of party leadership, government responsibility, social coordination, and public participation. Generally speaking, modern social management is not only a process in which the government provides public services to society and regulates relevant social affairs according to law, but is also a process of self-service and self-regulation and adjustment according to law and morality. These two processes complement each other and indispensable – they cannot substitute each other. Therefore, the construction of a modern social management system contains two basic objectives: on the one hand, it is necessary to continuously improve the government's social management ability and effectiveness; on the other hand, it is necessary to accelerate the self-development of society, enhancing the ability to self-manage society and expand social self-management.

**Scope:** in view of the current reality that the development of the Chinese society is clearly lagging behind, the establishment and realization of the second goal is particularly important. Participation in social governance is not only about civil society organizations relative to the state and government.

**Reform and improve** the government's social management system. The main affairs of modern government social management are public social affairs that cannot be handled by citizens, families, grassroots autonomous communities or non-profit social organizations. These social affairs involve the interests of the whole society.

**Social autonomy and self-management** should be vigorously developed. Social autonomy and self-management – composed of community self-governing organizations, non-profit social organizations and the majority of citizens – are two major components of the modern social management system.

The problem facing the reform and innovation of China's social management system is that the capacity for social self-development is still small. Compared with other, more powerful countries and markets, Chinese society is still in a weak position. The autonomy and self-management capabilities are insufficient, the conditions are limited and it is difficult to effectively undertake. The Chinese government has relatively withdrawn from its former social management functions and grassroots economic organisations. Therefore, China should vigorously develop and cultivate the social autonomy and self-management capabilities of the people.

**Extensively mobilize social resources.**
From international experience, there are three main sources of social resource investment in social management:
1.  the internal social management input of various institutions, such as corporate social investment as a part of modern corporate social responsibility.
2.  a society of various non-profit organizations. By investing, these organizations also partially self-sustain and develop through non-profit paid services after launch.
3.  various forms of social donations, including charitable donations.

**China should vigorously cultivate and develop human resources for professional social management.**

Professional social management human resources first of all refers to the talent team employed in various professional fields of social management, mainly from relevant government departments, public social service agencies, social organizations and community organizations, grassroots community self-governing organizations and non-profit civil society organizations. At present, the total number of professional social management personnel employed in these institutions in China is estimated to be about 40 million. They are the backbone of a professional social management human resources system.

Socialized social management of human resources also refers to those who participate in social management in various non-professional ways. Representatives are various volunteer teams. At present, volunteer teams play an increasingly important role in social management but socialized social management human resources are not limited to volunteer teams. There's a long way to go to adjust social interest relations, to regard society itself as the resolution of conflicts, to improve civic quality, to develop new social norms and civic awareness. Social supervision of social management work requires the broad participation of all citizens.

Professional social management of human resources mainly refers to the construction of professional social work talent pools, as well as the professionalization of social management talents. The two main ways to train professional social work talents and professional social management talents are: to train through the regular education system, the other is to strengthen on-the-spot relevant training.

**Technological innovations, improving the life of the elderly:**

One of the main issues in the elderly health sector is that many elders may faint or experience cardiovascular problems without anyone noticing due to them being alone. Once the elderly citizen is taken to a hospital hours or days after, it might already be too late for adequate or full recovery. In Jiangsu Street, Shanghai, engineers and community workers installed intelligent devices on the taps of elderly people's kitchens. The idea is to track whether said elderly has gone to drink within the past 12 hours. If the amount of water that has been used is less than 0.01 cubic meters or the frequency of use is beneath a certain threshold, an alarm will notify the community workers. Following the alarm, medical centres nearby or family members can be contacted immediately for help as soon as possible. A similar idea regarding the front door of their houses is being introduced which may take place in the future. These are all examples of innovation and technological developments made purely in service of citizens. Whilst the idea of water tracking is very basic and simple in terms of the censor and coding, the difficulty is having people on the other end that can track all the data. The people in charge of the alarms must be on 24/7 standby constantly and this can be a considerable hassle. However, with the right management, these ideas can be beautifully implemented and can pave the way for future ideas of the same nature. These contributions have been praised on social media and locally. China's government will undoubtedly contribute to this movement either by providing funding or other forms of support such as legislations.

小心
脚下
文学
Tianjin Binhai Library

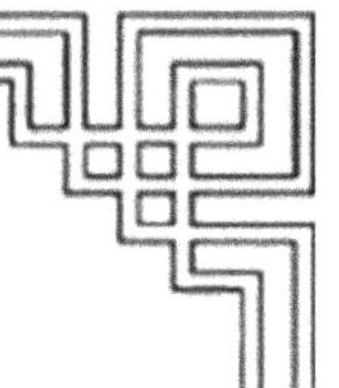

# Grid Management in Urban Communities.

*#grid #management #communities #optimization #urban*

*Urban community grid management constantly demonstrates its efficiency at promoting social harmony and a comprehensive and objective understanding of its value will help to further promote community governance reform and improve its effectiveness. There are three key advantages of grid management in urban communities: Clear jurisdiction and rational grid divisions, a continuously improving information service platform and improvement of interdepartmental collaboration. At the same time, there are defects to be improved: a shortage of full-time grid management staff, weak participation and awareness from residents. The management system can be optimised through changing the concept, strengthening the service level and improving the enthusiasm of residents.*

This chapter is important due to the way the upsides and potential downfalls of grid management are highlighted. When large infrastructural ideas emerge, many factors must be taken into account. However, ultimately China has found a way to smoothly transition into more effective systems as time went on.

**Why urban communities are keen on grid management.**[119]

Urban community grid management, as one of the major achievements of community management model innovation, constantly demonstrates its advantages in closely connecting with the people, improving the efficiency of community management work and promoting social harmony. However, with the increasing diversification of the needs of the people in the new era, the community grid management construction is also facing a series of new challenges. It is necessary to take corresponding countermeasures to actively respond.

---

119 Chinese Science and Technology Journal Database, *People's Forum, Ganlu Han Yu School of Politics and Public Administration, Xinjiang University*, No. 13 of 2018

## Urban community grid management, optimization path

Urban community grid management mode is one of the main means of grassroots community governance. It relies on unified urban management and a digital platform to divide urban management jurisdiction into unit grids according to certain standards. By strengthening the inspection of components and events of the grid cell, a way of management that separates and supervises the constituent elements is established. A comprehensive and objective understanding of the value of grid management will help to further promote community governance reform and improve governance effectiveness.

## The main advantages of grid management in urban communities

Clear jurisdiction and rational grid divisions.
Rational grid division is the basis for effective implementation of community grid management. Urban communities should establish community grid maps that are refined to the street level according to the actual situation of the number of residents, distribution characteristics and geographical location of the areas under their jurisdiction. On this basis, the effective deployment of full-time personnel to register and check the remediation status of the grid, and report problems in a timely manner can be achieved to determine the management focus. This initiative has made the original decentralized management structure more systematic and orderly, effectively improving management efficiency, increasing service density and improving service quality. At the same time, the grid management mechanism can optimize the emergency response mechanism based on the full understanding of the people's demands, providing early warning of social contradictions and

reasonably resolving contradictions, which is of great significance for maintaining social stability.

A continuously improving information service platform.
Today, with the rapid development of information technology, the intelligent community governance model is further popularized. Today, 'e-government', 'digital city' and 'smart city' are gradually applied to social governance and 'network elements' are continuously integrated into community grid management. Most communities have adopted interactive network platforms such as having a community WeChat public number, a community microblog and the developing mobile apps to establish a multi-dimensional information platform with extensive coverage. At the same time, grid management personnel are equipped with mobile security patrol network terminal equipment to share information in real-time. This measure facilitates the community in providing services to residents in a targeted manner and avoids restrictions on management by factors such as time and geography; it makes the communication feedback channel smoother.
Community residents can obtain community announcement information, respond to community information supervision departments and provide feedback on services through mobile devices. Grid management staff and community-related staff can also respond to residents' demands and handle community affairs in a timely manner through this platform, adjusting the service plan, providing a community zero-distance service in various ways, streamlining and compressing the tedious task handling in the community management system, greatly improving the efficiency of transaction processing and problem solving and improving the past chaos, inaction and slow service.

Inter-departmental collaboration is improving. The Urban

community grid management system fully draws on the characteristics of the 'flat management' structure, sets up relevant functional departments and manages and supervises 'two-axis' in parallel. In the process of managing and serving the residents of the community, the more difficult issues are reported to the next level in a timely manner, effectively achieving a two-way interaction. The grid management mechanism further integrates horizontal functional departments, breaks through the boundaries between functional departments, effectively unblocks the communication channels of various management units in the community, realizes information exchange, strengthens the links between departments and continuously improves the horizontal cooperation ability among various functional departments. It greatly improves the efficiency of social management. In addition, the grid management system effectively reduces the administrative burden. Its dual-axis management system further clarifies the responsibility of command management, supervision and evaluation of the participating entities. The work functions of each responsible department are also reasonably divided on the basis of this, so that each responsible entity performs its duties and effectively improves work efficiency.

**Optimization path of Urban community grid management.**

**First of all, we must further change the concept.** To advance the grid management of urban communities, we must continue to transform the old management concepts. It is necessary to pay more attention to grid management work in order to meet the needs of the people. Serving the people is an important prerequisite for effective management. Community work should focus on providing quality services to residents and solving practical problems in people's lives. It is necessary to completely transform the previous top-down administrative management model and implement a 'people-oriented' concept into community health care, education and public services, conveniences and other aspects; fully mobilize the enthusiasm of the various participants, as well as continuing to improve service levels and service quality to meet the demands of community residents. Alongside this, it is necessary to promote the Urban community grid management service team to effect diversified and professional development for community residents, non-governmental organizations, enterprises and other social forces in order that they participate in social governance and strengthen comprehensive performance abilities, with particular emphasis on differentiating services provided to residents in order to fill the gaps in the provision of services that have been existed in traditional management structures.

**Secondly, we must strengthen the service level** of full-time managers, continuously improving the service level of grid managers to ensure the effective operation of grid management in urban communities. The community needs to pay more attention to the induction and training of managers. First of all, it is necessary to regularly and professionally train existing staff, updating information technology knowledge and enhancing their business capabilities. Second, it is important to increase efforts to introduce talented people into grid management. In addition, because some grid managers are not as well-treated as employees of the same age in other professions and the promotion opportunities are limited, it is difficult to attract outstanding professionals into this position, which seriously affects the stability of the grid management team. Therefore, it is necessary to establish corresponding incentive mechanisms to enhance the enthusiasm and initiative of grid managers.

**Finally, we must improve the enthusiasm of residents** to participate in grid management. The participation of residents is the basis for the advancement of grid management in urban communities. In the process of promoting grid management, it is necessary to give full play to its advantages of mobilizing the residents and closely contacting the people, continuously improving the relevant mechanisms for open community affairs and providing convenient services for residents. To achieve this, it is necessary to regularly hold community meetings, organize residents to discuss community affairs, listen to their opinions and suggestions and use this as a basis to improve management and enhance residents' awareness of participation. Furthermore, to contribute to social governance, efforts should be made to deepen the construction of residents' participation in community affairs decision-making platforms, broaden the channels of participation and encourage community activists, stalwarts and residents. In addition, the community also needs to promote the spirit of service, strengthen the volunteer team, guide volunteer activities with standardized policies and create a good atmosphere of mutual help and mutual assistance.

Yingliang Stone Natural History Museum

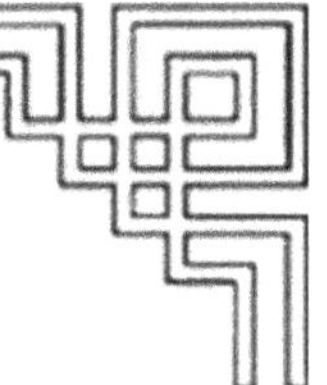

# Difficulties and Solutions with Grid Management.

*#grid-management #issues #solutions*

*Grid management emerged as an innovative method of urban governance since the 1980s to break through the shortcomings of current administrative departments. There are, however, difficulties with the grid management model: regional differences between the grids, deviations in the grid management objectives, limited channels for fundraising at the grassroots level, an imperfect intervention mechanism. The improvements to the system are as follows: build a work pattern with the participation of multiple entities, promote grid management according to local conditions, broaden the channels for fundraising, strengthen the grid management information network, and construct the talent team.*

Not only is it important for the grid ideas to be understood, but also the history helps provide context into why and how these creative ideas took off. This chapter delinquently discusses the past and now present ways of looking at grid systems. After all, many different eyes had to gaze these issues in order for an ideal idea to come out on top.

## Difficulties and countermeasures in the current wănggé huà guănlĭ - 'grid management' system.

Recently, along with the rapid urbanization process in China, the reform and innovation of urban social management has gradually become a hot topic of concern to all sectors of society. The 'grid management' governance method with digital city construction, technicalization of government social governance and urban management system reform has gradually been promoted nationwide. Although 'grid management' has been regarded as a new social governance strategy by the political and urban management circles, there are some areas of practice to be discussed.

## First, the reason for the 'grid management' mode

Since the founding of the People's Republic of China in 1949, in
the process of transforming China to a modern country, a 'general
society' governance structure was established, a 'state-to-dānwèi-
to-individual' system. The 'state-unit-individual' model is a vertical
linkage mobilization and control mechanism, that is, dānwèi (unit)
members rely on dānwèi organizations, which are organizational
means for the government to implement social mobilization and
control of society. Under this mechanism, the problem of urban
social management has been weakened to the utmost extent, because
the dānwèi system, by virtue of its 'unity' characteristics, combines
political, economic, social and cultural elements to form resource
allocation. A closed fortress with social integration. The dānwèi with
its government agencies, enterprises and institutions as the core, has
always been at the centre of society. A large number of social affairs
are basically handled by the dānwèi themselves, forming a pattern of
units running a society. Since the 1980s, essentially because of the
dominance of economic developments, the dānwèi system that has
continued for more than 30 years has begun to erode.

## Second, the operation of the 'grid management' mode.

At present, most of China's grid management model is based on
streets and communities. In the management area, the grid is divided
into units based on the area of about 10000 square meters. A grid
management information platform is established, based on that
entity, alongside component and event implementation management,
a management mode and information resource sharing system with
four levels of connection (between city, district, professional disposal
department and grid supervisor).

The purpose of implementing grid management is to break through the shortcomings of the current administrative departments. Shortcomings such as fragmentation, individual politics, arbitrage and unclear rights and re-integration resources.

In this sense, the core of 'gridization' is not just to add a smaller level of the basic management unit, but to rewrite the institutional structure of basic social management. Along with the complexity of urban management and the increase in the number of tasks, the administrative bureaucracy is facing tremendous management pressure and has to actively promote its own transformation from management to governance.

## Third, the difficulties faced with the 'grid management' model

Through consulting large datasets and consultations with grassroots staff, it appears that there are chiefly the following problems in the practice of grid management in China. Note that the scope of issues outlined is limited to urban communities only. Rural communities may face other issues.

**3. 1. Regional differences between the grids**. Since 'grid management' is still in the exploratory stage in China and lacks mature experience, many regions cannot be inducted into a process that is suitable for all local conditions, flexible and orderly and meeting the standards of proper grid management. The multi-intervention and organizational form of the administrative colour is strong and it is inevitable that some problems will arise. What needs to be given particular consideration is that some large and medium-sized cities or megacities have large geographical areas, large populations, complex residential structures, diverse social organizations, economic development status, group structures, functional positioning and industrial layouts while in urban core areas, there is the issue of functional development areas, new development areas and suburbs. There are big differences and the task of social governance is arduous. It is generally difficult for each region to take care of the characteristics of the region in the implementation process of grid management.

**3.2. Deviations in the grid management objectives.**
To some extent, grid management overemphasizes the innovation of information technology and methods and ignores the core objectives of community management and services. Too much emphasis on the search for innovative applications of instrumental methods, plus simple and rigid control, has brought negative effects to the promotion of grassroots democracy and community autonomy; the focus of grid management is then on trivial matters such as work planning or issuing permits.

**3.3. Limited channels for fund-raising at grassroots level.**
Grid management requires not only hardware investment, such as purchasing required equipment (mobile phones, laptops, …), building IT networks, etc., but also the ownership of community buildings, public security, family planning, health care, cultural and sports activities, equipment maintenance, hiring and training, etc. Unfortunately, at the grassroots level, especially at the community level, the ability to raise funds is limited. The economic level of each city is uneven, each situation is different, there is no effective fund-raising mechanism and the financing channels are limited. The current grid management funds still rely mainly on government input and community.

**3.4. An imperfect incentive mechanism.**
Grid management should mobilize all parties to participate in a wide range of activities, optimize, integrate and share resources, thereby

improving the quality and efficiency of management and services. However, in the actual grid management, due to the imperfect incentive mechanism, relying solely on administrative orders and simple marketing, it is impossible to fully mobilize the enthusiasm of residents to participate in community autonomy.

## Fourth, improve the measures of grid management

### 4.1. Build a work pattern with participation of multiple entities.

It is important to vigorously support and nurture social organizations, guide the growth of social grassroots organizations, mobilize the enthusiasm of social organizations to actively participate in self-government, regulate the activities and management mechanisms of social organizations through institutional constraints, give social organizations more autonomy and disperse individual residents. The integration of interest claims has risen to the common rationalization appeal of the organization and as far as possible, reflects the overall demands of the society at policy level.

### 4.2. Promote grid management according to local conditions.

It is preferable that the county-level government will instigate the various communities to explore the feasible path for grid management in a phased, hierarchical and sub-regional manner and move in a way which is flexible and orderly. For areas with an underdeveloped economy or a complex population structure, it is necessary to appropriately strengthen the guidance, demonstration and leading role of the government to ensure the steady reform and innovation of community grid management on the basis of harmony and stability. It is contributing to a faster development of economic and social organisations.

## 4.3. Broaden the channels for fund raising.

For the management and service of projects that the market
can afford, they decisively should go their own way without
any government intervention. In case there are NGOs that are
hesitating to invest or lack the capacity, the government could
provide temporary start capital or investment and encourage the
community to actively participate in community construction and
development. There should also be comprehensive use of various
fiscal and tax incentives to enhance the attractiveness of investment
in community management and services, as well as the establishment
and improvement of relevant policies and regulations; legal
protections for community financial fund-raising and rational use
should be provided. It should also be incumbent to make full use of
the advantages of the community, standardize the community fund-
raising mechanism, extensively absorb the idle funds of society and
continuously enhance the self-accumulation of the community and
the ability to raise funds.

## 4.4. Strengthen the grid management information network.

According to the requirements of community management and
service, all services are included in a unified system framework, not
only in the hardware infrastructure, but also in software maintenance,
to optimize and upgrade, to form a complete and standardized
information city community management system. It is necessary to
incorporate household, civil affairs, economy, party and government,
family planning, social security, public security and many other
contents into the grid management interactive platform and assign
permissions according to the division of work between the street
workers, community staff and grid management personnel to form a
real-time, online and shared network platform.

Qinglongwu Zhejiang Capsule Boutique
Hotel and Library

# Grid Management: a Case Study.

*#grid management #security #measurements #society #test-cases*

Both the government and the people will inevitably compare systems to the current or previous counterparts. This is not necessarily a bad habit, as it can trigger more critical critique of the current system and open way for new creative solutions. The Baojia system for example is a common comparison with the grid management.

Recently, the Shanghai Hongkou district began piloting integrated grid management services, coordinating community parliamentary offices, service centres for the elderly and social organization service centres, so that residents can get a settlement of their issues <u>within fifteen minutes</u>. The pilot project of gridded comprehensive services in the Hongkou district is essentially a combination of grassroots grid governance and a community 'one-stop service' (POC, Single Point of Contact), reflecting the innovation of grassroots social governance.

From a nationwide perspective, the grid-based governance innovation model is diverse and it is of great significance for realizing the social governance pattern proposed by the Fifth Plenary Session of the 18th CPC Central Committee to build a nation-wide joint, common system. However, there are still some misunderstandings in society about grid governance. For example, some people keep thinking that grid governance is actually a variant of the dānwèi ('maintain stability') system. Others think it is a system imported from developed countries. To resolve the confusion in understanding of the purpose of grid governance, it is necessary to distinguish and clarify from a historical perspective.

**Grid governance is essentially different from the Republican era' Baojia system:**

During the time of the Republic of China (1912 - 1949), the Republicans proposed a 'guarantee system'. The target time for the law proposal to be tested by was August 1932. In the promulgation of the *Regulations on the registration of the Baojia Hùkǒu in the counties in the reclamation area* for the Uyghur, Henan and Anhui provinces it is clearly stated that three provinces (Hubei, Henan and Anhui) would apply for establishment for a limited period. After several years, the Baojia system was gradually opened in some Kuomintang districts. In November 1934, the *Regulations on Local Self-Government Laws* stipulated that the Baojia township organization would be housed in the autonomous region organization. In that way, the regulation of the 'guarantee system' was officially established. However, this seemingly standardized grassroots governance creation would end soon after. The reason, fundamentally speaking, was that it failed to effectively form an organized network, it actually linked the interests of the management and thus departs from the people.

**First of all,** from a formal point of view, the access threshold of the Baojia system was too high. Actually, people were rejected from the door of the Baojia. The benefits in the Baojia system were not available to the average person.

**Secondly,** from a functional point of view, the Baojia system's establishment was not to maintain social stability — its original intention was to eliminate the Red Army. The new Baojia system's purpose was to establish a front line for the Kuomintang anti-communist regime in Jiangxi Province. The infamous 'Baojia Hukou Regulations' and 'Baojia Training Order' previously mentioned were to establish a Baojia system along the revolutionary base areas. In fact, the reason why the Baojia system was implemented between 1932 and 1934 was precisely to cooperate with the Kuomintang's main force to encircle the Red Army as a supporting programme. In the first half of 1933, the Kuomintang began to use the so-called 'Bunker Strategy' as proposed by the Germans to encircle the Red Army. From 1937 onwards, the Baojia were used not only to control the Red Army, but also the Japanese infiltrations.

**The current grid governance is not a model originating from the governance of developed countries.** In fact, as early as the 1930s, the Communist Party has pioneered grassroots grid governance.

In November 1933, when the Republican government established the Baojia system at the border area with Russia, Mao Zedong led, in preparation of the second National Soviet Congress report, the Soviet inspection team to Changgang and Caixi Township for investigation. At that time, political frustrations did not make Mao Zedong depressed. Instead, he urged party members to understand the grassroots situation through field visits and research. Based on a survey, he wrote the *Changgang and Caixi Township Survey* **reports. During that investigation, party members asked them the question why the enthusiasm couldn't be entirely mobilized in the same way as in Changgang and Caixi Township.**

In short, the experience of grassroots management in Changgang and Caixi Township was the discovery that one of the most important lessons was to divide the entire territory of the township into several small villages, so people could rely on their own township representatives and village committees. The strong leadership of the people in the village enabled the entire village to be organized like a network. In other words, people in a network can maximize profound changes with a noble spirit and enthusiasm. This is the most important lesson from the establishment of grid management in Changgang and Caixi Township.

**The specific practices of Changgang and Caixi Townships:**

**Firstly**, the establishment of various teams or committees to achieve administrative autonomy. This involved incorporating as many people as possible into the committee and making them participate in social changes. Take Changgang Township as an example: there were 437 villagers and 1785 people in the township. They established 15 committees, including an expansion of the Red Army Committee, teams and workgroups for land registration, forests, water conservancy and bridges, state-owned property, warehouse custody, education, a health committee, etc. As much as possible, each household was encouraged to become a committee member, so that the people themselves could be truly become 'masters of the family'.

**The second stage** was to establish cooperatives to achieve agricultural production autonomy. Cooperatives included model farming teams, labour mutual aid agencies and ploughing cattle cooperatives, mobilizing farmers' enthusiasm for agricultural production as much as possible and improving agricultural production efficiency.

**The third stage** was to establish local troops and militia organizations to achieve armed defence and autonomy. The militia organizations in Changgang Township included a team of male Red Guards, a team of female Red Guards and a small team of foreigners.

**In summary**, through the cross-combination of committees, cooperatives and militia organizations, almost everyone in Changgang and Caixi Township was included in a network-like organization system with sufficient active members. Inactive people could also become members of the organization under the cross-organization of the grid system, thus maximizing the enthusiasm for the autonomy of the organization. In this regard, the report stated: "The characteristic of Changgang Township's work is to use all efforts to mobilize the people and use great patience to persuade the people, they are fully able to realize their tasks."[120]

**Two key inspirations:**
**First**, the grid governance has been tried and has succeeded in the past— almost one century ago.
**Second**, the biggest secret of the success of grid governance is the close contact with the people.

**Lessons learned:**
Based on the 'Ruijing experience', where should attention be paid in the future of grassroots grid governance in China? The key is to avoid two bad trends:

**The first is to avoid the formalization and bureaucratization of grid governance.** In some places, people still misunderstand the purpose of grid governance itself. The lessons of history tell us that close contact with the people, rather than the government, is the magic weapon for the success of grid governance in the practice of

---

120  The Foreign Agents Registration Act, 22 U.S.C. § 611 et seq. (FARA)
https://www.justice.gov/nsd-fara

grassroots social governance. It is precisely because of the practice of grid governance in some places that there is no real consideration from the perspective of the residents. There is no specific method for designing grids for the vital interests of the residents, so that a very small number of grassroots cadres themselves will be gridded. The specific work is seen as a form and a task that has to be done, so that the coming together of these aspects may be in the most appropriate manner.

**The second is to avoid places where grid governance evolves into 'grid governance people' rather than 'human grid governance'.** The key is to keep close contact with residents. If the grid governance is separated from the people, it will make the grid governance external to people, becoming a separate way of living and make the grid becoming a tool to restrain people, bind people and even restrict people's free development. Therefore, it is necessary to closely keep in contact with the people in the process of grid governance, <u>so that the cadres worship the residents</u> like a bodhisattva and let them become the main body of grid governance rather than being subject to grid governance.

To put it bluntly, if the grid governance is a bone, then the people are blood. Only if the bones are borne in blood will the bones have vitality to grow. Otherwise, it will only have its own form and will eventually be eliminated by history.

> A powerful failure, because it is separated from the people;
> a small victory, because it connects with the people.
>
> Mao Zedong

Xiaomutang Childrens Teaching Restaurant

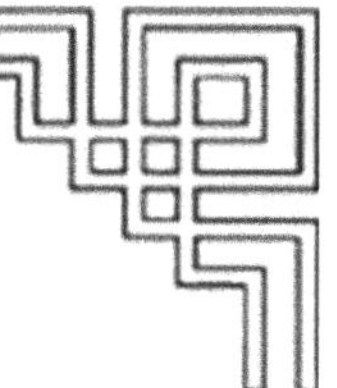

# Policy Basis for Grid Management.

*#grid-management #politics #basis #reform*

The grid management is important to understand because not only is it operating on a central level, it is tailor made in many ways for local areas. Meaning that, the base idea is from the central government, however, the speciality of each case will depend on the local region. Therefore, each local area must have a good understanding of their system and the flaws of it.

**Wang Jiexiu, in his report on the situation of 'promoting the modernization of the community governance system and governance capacity':**

For the first time, on 8th November 2012, the 18th National Congress of the Communist Party of China [121] wrote *urban and rural community governance* into the party's programme documents, requiring people's self-management t, self-service, self-education and self-monitoring in urban and rural community governance. The Third Plenary Session of the 18th CPC Central Committee proposed: 'innovative social governance system', 'improving social governance methods' and promoting the reform tasks of 'urban and rural community governance', forming a governance system that integrates national governance, social governance and community governance. The Fourth Plenary Session of the 18th CPC Central

---

121  18th National Congress of the Communist Party of China
https://en.wikipedia.org/wiki/18th_National_Congress_of_the_Communist_Party_of_China

---

Committee further clarified that it is necessary to accelerate the construction of a legal system for the innovation of social governance systems and promote multi-level and multi-disciplinary governance.

**Political basis for grid management:**[122]

The decision of the Third Plenary Session of the 18th Central Committee on comprehensively deepening the reform of some major issues on 12th November 2013 proposed to improve the social governance system, innovate the social governance system and to improve the grassroots integrated service management platform in the direction of grid management and socialized services.

**Core functions of grid management:**

**Basics.**

It is mainly up to grid staff to carry out comprehensive information collection and management of the five elements (people, places, material, events and organization) within the jurisdiction, collecting geographical location, community buildings, houses, unit stores, population information, civil remedies, community building, discipline inspection, trade union work, family planning, labour security, comprehensive treatment information and visits, township characteristics, volunteer services, market shops, safe production, special population, public security information and fire safety information.

---

122  Wang Jiexiu 2015.07.27
Promoting the modernization of the community governance system
http://www.mca.gov.cn/article/zwgk/hyzb/20150700854665/index.html

## Statistical analysis platform

It is of vital importance to summarize and analyse all kinds of data and information in the database in a smart way, to generate digital, graphical reports and to use a histogram and pie chart to show a status report of the grid at a glance, highlight the key points and analyse the whole.

## Assessment appraisal platform

Basically, this is a management assessment conducted by a superior of the performance during a given time period. In that way, the system can automatically rank the various grid organizations at all levels.

The content of the assessment is about the time required to handle an incident, the number of incidents and the quality of the diary of the grid personnel, including an appraisal of the quality of incident assessment.

Assessment is an important part of the system and useful as a long-term mechanism. It needs to be formulated in all its details depending on the actual situation. Everything and everyone is to be assessed and has an accountability mechanism.

## Geographic information platform

The electronic geographic information (GPS) platform supports the annotation of information such as districts, streets and communities on two-dimensional maps and satellite maps. It supports the marking of buildings, houses and other information on a multi-layer, three-dimensional map. It automatically connects with the population database; it displays all buildings including the data of the residents in each building, giving information on households as well as the heads of households and family members.

The three-dimensional map display is a combination of digital city model technologies of the actual process, showing the urban style and regional divisions. The map information platform displays all the buildings of a certain community or compound including each apartment in each building.

## GPS positioning platform

The GPS function of the positioning of grid staff can show in real-time the location monitoring of grid staff based on its handheld mobile terminal. After the command centre logs into the system, they select a specific organization. The position of the corresponding personnel can be displayed at the corresponding organization level.

**Examples and case studies:**

**1. The innovative digital information system for social governance of Weidu district, Xuchang city, Henan province.**

The grid management of Weidu district aims to 'go the extra mile to serve the people and regards social governance innovation as the first priority project in the whole district. The district integrates the administrative management service resources for the whole district. Based on the morning grid management system, it strengthens the district, street, community and grid four-level services and establishes the mass appeal service and security in the district, office and community. The information-based social governance service platform, integrating control, convenience service and emergency command has opened a specific hotline service for the Weidu district residents. The 24/7, full coverage collects and resolves the issues reflected by the people.

In order to address the issue of hesitation when it came to reporting directly to the social governance top grid management team, as well solve the less-obvious, invisible issues, the district divided the whole district into 408 grids.

Each grid has a grid plan, a grid administrator, a civil information officer, a grid police officer and a grid supervisor. The capacity to deal with the occasionally contradictory mediation between public services and similar matters is integrated into the grid system. The grid is equipped with a handheld grid mobile phone, which can capture, collect and report problems at any time to the information platform. The most enthusiastic people in the community acted as informants and grid supervisors; they became the eyes to find the source of the case and give feedback, they're the tentacles of law enforcement. Informatization and gridding effectively solve the problem of segmentation, information shielding, mutual deduction and responsibility avoidance between departments.

## 2. The operation mode of 'one meeting, one book and one order' in Baita district, Liaoyang city, Liaoning province.

Baita district in Liaoyang city activated community resources and strengthened community service functions to further innovate the community service model and improve the community service network. The district also vigorously promoted grid management as per the 'one-on-one-one-one-one' operation mode in each community.

In the big grid of the street, the sub-grid of the community and the grid unit (the compound), the 'one-on-one-one-one-one-one-one-one-people' work-management method was implemented. A so called 'one-seven-seven-member' service mode is standardized so that active detection and timely processing can be improved. It also enhances the service management capabilities.

The 'One Meeting' is the grid agenda meeting; no other separate meetings are allowed. Within the meeting, service events in the 'three-level grid' are researched, analysed and solved. There are also proposals for outstanding issues and work suggestions which are referred to the upper-level grid agenda meeting.

## 3. The standard: the 'Diary of the People'.

The 'Diary of the People's Lives' is a daily record of the service activities of the grid staff, recording the time, place, service object, service form, service content, problems encountered, situation handling method, experience (lessons learned) and other aspects of each service. Each responsible department randomly checks the 'Diary of the People's Lives' from time to time and grasps the service of the grid staff as the basis for assessment.

'One Order' is the short name for the 'Grid Provider Service Report Form'. It is a form of registration: a full registration of grid staff services, etc. It systematically analyses and summarizes the different problems encountered by community residents in their lives, so that they can carry out targeted common services for the future which is a convenience for district committees and district governments. Human decision-making needs a scientific basis. Each responsible department collects the 'Grid Provider Service Report Forms' every month and masters the grid staff service status as the basis for the assessment and statistical analysis of the overall work service situation of the whole district.

The implementation of 'One Book, One Meeting and One Order' in the workflow makes grid management and grid management services more standardized and refined. The morning grid management system is conducive to the integration of community resources, improving work efficiency and improving service standards. As a result of this, the style of community work gets more solid, contradictions are resolved in a more timely fashion, the security line is more solid, the order of letters and visits is more standardized and service users are more satisfied. It plays an important role and significance in strengthening urban grassroots social management, promoting the construction of harmonious communities and improving the community management system.

**4. An incentive to all departments to improve quality**, including family planning, production safety, fire management, petitioning letter and visit stability , community correction, school campus and the surrounding environment, key fire-fighting sites and culvert water conservancy facilities. This represents a fast improvement in terms of work requirements due to the gridded model, standardization and standardized management.

The Wuling Social Governance Grid Integrated Information Platform is connected with the province's family planning department's population information platform; therefore, it is possible to access and exchange large data sets and share resources of mass information.

Xianju Paper-cut Art Workshop and
Lakeside Libraries

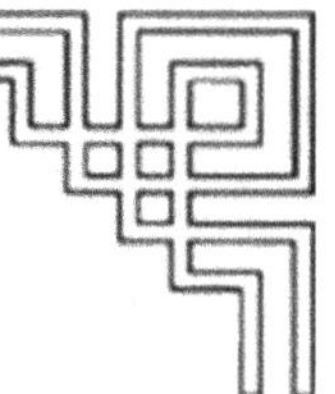



# Pressing Questions about Grid Management.

*#issues #problems #questions #solutions*

Grid management can be used for many purposes. In the past these living complexes have been used as a tool for dictatorship or control. Therefore, it is essential for the population to understand and willingly accept these systems into their areas. To understand the root intentions of the government is often what can stop corruption or abuse.

## 1. Is 'grid management' a return to the 'guarantee system'?

Grid management is not the return of the old 'guarantee system' (the 保甲 bǎojiǎ or the more recent 维稳 wéiwěn).

The root of the bǎojiǎ system can be traced back to the Song dynasty. It has evolved since then and has changed several times. Later, because the Kuomintang government used the bǎojiǎ system as a grassroots administrative organization system under the county level to maintain its power, the bǎojiǎ system was overshadowed by a serious class division.

Considered objectively, the bǎojiǎ was one of the three cornerstones of rural autonomy maintenance in an agrarian society. Throughout China's history, the bǎojiǎ system has been fundamental. The bǎojiǎ organization can be said to be a social grassroots organization with

Chinese historical characteristics. The government's contact with the grassroots people and the management of contemporary grassroots societies have been enabled by establishing a form of social management organisation that also proved to be the basis of a stable existence of the imperial power.

Compared with the bǎojiǎ organization, the neighbourhood and village committees, which were established in China during the 1980s have not been completely abolished and reconstructed. There are indeed some similarities. Fengqiao town's[123] earliest grid management was set up to establish a management extension and responsibility for the two village committees through a comprehensive management grid, maximizing the use of rural connections to intervene in issues regarding stability control and mediation. Obviously, a grid management system with the single purpose of maintaining stability is questionable. Today, most academics regard it as a stage dictatorship tool. But as scholars have pointed out, the choice of rural governance systems in different periods serves the political goals of different countries at that time period. After 1950, in villages in rural areas as well as in urban districts, various models of community organizations have been tried out to promote and encourage self-governance. Moreover, at present, 'grid management' is not simply a tool for the 'dictatorship by the people'[124]; it pays much more attention to the service to the people, making it essentially different from the Baojia system.

---

123  Fengqiao (枫桥, literally "Maple Bridge") a township in Zhuji city, Zhejiang province 枫桥经验 (fēngqiáo jīngyàn) The "Fengqiao experience":
http://sfj.sh.gov.cn/info/f79703a95de640ac9b7d6d2e6a6f9d51
124  "people's democratic dictatorship" in Chapter 1, Article 1 of The Constitution of the People's Republic of China 20.10.2019
http://en.people.cn/constitution/constitution.html

## 2. Does 'grid management' contradict the cultivation of a civil society?

I believe that as long as the correct implementation of grid management is the means, community-based service is the purpose. Grid management should not simply used as a means of prevention and control, but more as a way of innovative service to the people. Up to now, grid management has contributed to the cultivation of a civil society. Through the original comprehensive management network and the current broader group network, nearly 10% of the urban population has participated in community governance, either as information workers, mediators, volunteers or grid service team members. The lessons learned from Fengqiao prove to a certain extent that China with its collectivist tradition is fundamentally different from Western countries that advocate individualism. China's civil society is hardly spontaneous in the same way as the Western civil society, but it should be more leveraged. Formed in a collective spirit, the 'grid management, group-based service' happens to be a collectively diversified and colourful method; it is a civil society cultivation method with Chinese characteristics.

## 3. Is the high investment 'grid management' of Fengqiao town universal?

High investment is only a relative concept. Professor Li Peilin[125] proposed that at present, China has certain conditions to meet for the needs of social management resources input – currently the key is a rational allocation of public resources. In the past few years, Fengqiao Town has not been extravagant with its grid management. During this time, the investment for the implementation of

---

125  Li Peilin 李培林, "Innovative social management, a new task of China's reform." https://www.en84.com/fy/fwx/qita/5465.html

comprehensive management work funds for the accessibility approval was an average annual funding of four million yuan (It was in fact, the first city to implement the concept of rational allocation of public finance). Today, the public finance investment all tends to go towards social management.

In addition, in Fengqiao town, the social coherence benefits far outweigh the costs. The annual average of four million yuan for comprehensive management work in Fengqiao town only accounts for 1.4% of the total fiscal revenue, but it helps to obtain multiple benefits: sustained economic growth, social harmony and stability, and high satisfaction among the residents. Moreover, these gains are only the explicit gains in the short and medium term. In the future, making use of the currently unrevealed income in the medium and long term, the model of social stability and economic development in Fengqiao town will further progress.

Chongqing Xinhua Bookstore

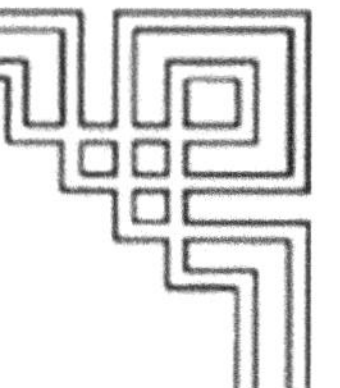



# Advantages of Grassroots Community Building.

*#grassroots #community building #standardisation*

*The grassroots community-building grid management offers various advantages and opportunities. This system was designed specifically for the needs of the people. With an organisational up and down levelling in the system, navigation and connections are widely available. Furthermore, many facilities are put in place to meet the desires of the public specifically.*

This chapter shines light on various interesting advantages that certain communities have. Understanding these advantages and collecting the reactions of people towards such services is a formula for greatness. Through effective communication and understanding, the grassroots community along with every grid system can drastically improve.

## Advantages of the new model of grassroots community building grid management[126]

**Zhengdong New Area, district of Zhengzhou city, Henan province** takes the service of the people as the starting point and foothold, further innovates the working mode of community building, actively explores the establishment of a new mode of grassroots community building and grid management, realizes clearer responsibilities of grassroots cadres, launches local activities, participates extensively and protects in a powerful way. With a refined management team, the service is more tailor-made and comprehensive, in order to offer more benefits to the people.

**Hengyang city, Hunan province.** The implementation of a new model of grassroots community building opened the way to better grid management and refined services, it established a community

---

126 Wang Sisi, "Advantages of the new model of grassroots community building" 12.04.2018
www.jpsycn.com

building mechanism that combines bar resources, resource sharing, complementary advantages, co-construction while always promoting grassroots organizations. It has innovated the ability and level of social management; it serves the people, promotes social harmony and social management of Hengyang with the community building grid.

**First, the organization settings gridding:** in response to a series of new situations and new problems, such as the difficulty in managing community members, the difficulties in functioning, the difficulties in carrying out activities and the difficulties in supervision within the community, Hengyang city actively explored, when developing the grid, the grid management of community building and the residents' community work grid. Management software, implementation opinions and former pilot projects in several urban areas, with the regional jurisdiction of townships and streets as a unit, set up a top-level grid with a secondary grid in the village (community). Below that second level, there's a third-level grid.

The system was set up considering the population based on the principles of close residence, easy management, easy gathering, convenient service and easy activities. At the same time, according to the standards of 'good quality, strong ability, high prestige, and place', the community manager is elected by the community or village members. By finetuning the community organization, the community cohesion building will be used to promote the autonomy of the residents and with the guidance of community members, the work of grassroots self-government should be further advanced.

**Second, the standardization of community members' management: wisdom in community building.** The dual management model (based on management of the community unit organization and supplemented by the management of the grid branch) implements a management system that combines and links up and down. After the implementation of the community building grid management, the cadre style was effectively transformed and the grassroots community building and other dynamics were mastered for the first time. The contradictions and disputes were resolved straight away, the role of community members was effectively defined and the relationship between the community people was more harmonious. After the participants visited the site, they were very impressed; they praised the approach.

**Third, the service to the people.** Convenient service halls will be built to provide a one-stop (SPC Single Point of Contact) service booth window. The aim is to improve the service facilities of village-level service centres, standardize the work system such as organising work-shifts in villages and improve the marketing of village education and culture. Another aim is to clearly define responsibilities, put the service for the people into practice and guide the cadres and community members to carry out activities by the volunteers: poverty alleviation, improving access to government services, ensuring close contact between the party and the people and assisting the people. Every grid manager should visit two to three households at least once per quarter. They aim to provide refined services to the people, enhancing the service level to the satisfaction of the residents and the grassroots community organizations.

The implementation of grassroots community building and grid management is the most important innovation and breakthrough of grassroots community building. The majority of grassroots community members should participate in most of the activities, take the initiative to claim the community member responsibility in the area, actively participate in volunteer service team, extensively carry out pairing assistance activities and give full play to the vanguard and exemplary role of community members. It is necessary to rely on the community building to be gridded, to strengthen the service to the residents, to innovate social management, to optimize public services and to set up employment opportunities, focusing on achieving small but practical results. The aim is to really let the community members gather in the grid and play their role in the grid.

Songyang Lishui Cultural Centre
and Library

# 34.

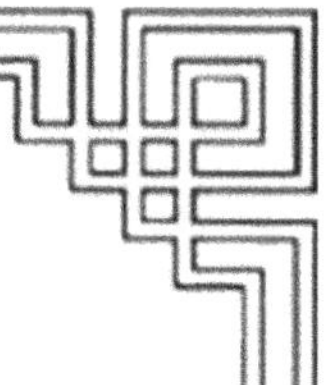

# China has a Bright Future.

*#China #future #unique #features*

*Within the next 50 years, China has various strategic fields to advance and flourish in. A new scenery of modern infrastructure, engineering and decision making while maintaining the classic Chinese ideals and traditions. Every facet of individual and group life will be improved financially, legally and socially. China has a lot of potential, and the growth is only starting.*

Effectively the last chapter of the book summarises and emphasises the reasons why China is heading for a bright future. This is extremely important to read whether the audience is Chinese or a foreigner. For Chinese people, this is reason to have hope and trust the process. For foreigners, this is informative information that destroys their previous misconceptions about China.

**Why China has a bright future. 25 arguments to take China into account for the next 50 years:**

**Efficient government:**

Compared to the reactive, slow, bureaucratic management of many EU countries, the Chinese government is forward-looking highly efficient.

**Excellent infrastructure:**

Highways, train tracks, subways, deep-sea ports. Everything brand new and suitably devised.

**Many well educated, smart engineers:**

No other country on this globe has so many smart, well-trained and devoted engineers.

**Strong motivation to work hard.**

Work motivation is a major problem in Western Europe. People are spoilt by social security systems and no longer feel the need to make extra efforts. HR is forced to select on motivation, rather than on professional experience. In China, most employees still want to make that extra effort when needed.

**A clear career plan:**

Chinese students, much more than Western students, have a clear plan for their professional future.

**Strong personal competition:**

The Chinese education system is strongly encouraging competition between students. The economic value of interpersonal competition is of inestimable importance.

**One-child policy, now two-child policy:**

Another strong stimulus for economic development. All efforts of Chinese parents are focused on their one child. Their child is the financial and economic future of their family.

**Guanxi:**

The Chinese way of networking, much more powerful than the Western way of networking.

## Confucianism:

Confucianism is back in China.

The Great Learning (大学 Dà Xué) and advanced knowledge are key tenets of Confucianism.

Confucius opposed egalitarianism; bringing the productive initiative of the people into full play by allocating work which is best suited to the individual's attributes. Separation of income and work.

## Strong family ties:

In China, family relations are strong and powerful. Family members have the moral duty to support each other financially.

Many small companies are based on financial support/investment of the extended family.

## Equal gender relations:

Men and women have almost equal education and career opportunities, a positive remnant of the May 4th movement in 1919.

No religious or other traditions, restricting the role of women in society. Many Chinese companies are managed or owned by women.

## Wide income gap:

An encouragement for hard work; a strong incentive for economic development.

**Healthy social and work climate:**

In Europe, labour unions do not hesitate to take company managers hostage. In China, employees fully understand that a business is intended to make money to pay their salaries.

**No religious extremism, no islamic violence:**

Companies can invest safely without having to fear religious nonsense, violence or robbery.

**Faith in the future, nationalism, a belief in building a better China:**

Chinese people have a strong believe in the future. They are prepared to sacrifice time and effort for their next generation.

**The new customers are in China:**

Gradually, Chinese customers have gained so much spending power that, today, they are buying more luxury products than any other country.

**A huge potential source of low salary workers:**

Contrary to all other Asian tigers or BRIC (Brazil, Russia, India and China) countries, China has a huge source of low salary workers. In the west of China, they can recruit assembly line workers for the next 15 years. And if that source is drying up, they'll find new workers in Africa.

**Business flexibility:**

Chinese companies are flexible beyond imagination. They can change products, management, focus or anything overnight.

**Decision power:**

In Europe and North America, companies are strictly organised – an Excel form for every action or decision. In Chinese companies, decisions are often made quickly and over the phone.

**Money:**

Chinese society is based on saving money. Many Chinese companies and families have substantial amounts of money in their bank account. All cars in China are paid for with cash. Consumer credit is almost non-existent. China as a country has almost no foreign debts.

**Smart people:**

In all my travels, all over this globe (I have been to 34 countries), I have nowhere else met so many smart, fast thinking people as in China. Not just students or professionals, but so many ordinary people. We have to admit it; they are just plain and simply smarter than we in the West.

**The sheer power of numbers:**

In 2010, there were 1.34 billion people in China, today almost 1.4 billion; that's more than the US and Europe combined. The domestic consumption of China is growing very fast.

## Human and cultural flexibility

China and the Chinese people have an incredible flexibility. Their culture has survived the Egyptians, the Greeks and the Romans. They certainly will also survive and even surpass our Western culture.

## The money mountain:

The huge number of rich people in China and the fast-growing economy is creating inevitable investment in western companies. In China, there is a growing confidence to buy or take over western businesses.

## Low salaries

This is still today a good reason why many Western companies go to China. It is the engine of the Chinese economy. Indeed, labour costs are rising in the coastal areas, but are still quite low elsewhere.

Huxi Sichuan Fine Arts Institute
and Library

# 35.

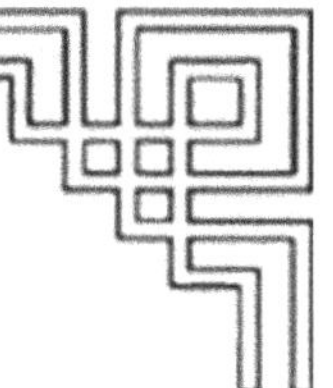

# Contributors, Acknowledgements.

*#contributors #acknowledgements #appreciation #thanks*

**My sincere thanks** go to everyone who inspired me to write this book. There are really too many to mention; I hope those I have forgotten with my scatter brain can forgive me.
**A special word of praise and appreciation for all the contributors who have provided me with ideas, directions and reports, all of which has led to the quality of this book:**

## China and the Chinese people

They have shaken up my life and have taught me who I am. Thank you China!

## David Wang 王首徫

Dean of the IIGS (International Institute on Governance and Strategy), an integrated high-end social think tank dedicated to international relations, theory and practice of national governance, social economic development, public policy and international security in areas such as research and analysis.

## Steven Bó Yuē 伯约

Europe Department manager at the Chinese Ministry of Commerce. For his contributions about grassroots organisations in China and substantial research reports from the China Rural Research Institute of the Central China Normal University in Wuhan.

## Wu Licai 吴理财 (via 伯约 Steven Bó Yuē) on 09.04.2019

Provided on-the-field information about 维稳 and 网格化管理

## Li Peilin 李培林

Author of *Innovative social management, a new task of China's reform.*

## Hu Fusun 胡福孙

Author of 梅花香自苦寒来 *Plum Blossom from the Bitter Cold.* A most beautiful book about 胡焕勇Hu Huanyong, his grandfather, a geographer and anthropologist, former dean of the Geography Institute of the Nanjing University, founder of the Heihe–Tengchong line, the Hu-line theory.

## Zhou Hui 周泂

Who has taught me the real China, the daily issues of life, China at grassroots level. My most sincere and profound thanks.

## Dao Tao

10 years' CPC member. Thank you for your frank and sincere attestation about the Communist Party.

## Gordon Dumoulin 杜墨

Fleming, entrepreneur, writer on China business and actualities. Gordon is living and running his own business in Beijing with corporate focus on various business culture management services. Thanks for his excellent contribution about *Philanthropy with Chinese Characteristics*.

## Godfree Roberts

Ed.D. Education and Geopolitics, University of Massachusetts, Amherst (1973)
for his various contributions and his deep insights in Chinese politics.

## Jeff J. Brown

Author of *44 Days, Doctor WriteRead's Treasure Trove to Great English* and his masterpiece *China Rising, Capitalist Roads, Socialist Destinations – The Truth behind Asia's Enigmatic Colossus.*
Jeff also authored *China Is Communist, Dammit! – Dawn of the Red Dynasty.* He is a contributing editor with the Greanville Post, Dispatch from Beijing, and is a Global Opinion Leader at 21st

Century. Jeff also writes columns for *The Saker*, called *the Moscow-Beijing Express*. He writes, interviews and podcasts on his own programme: *China Rising Radio Sinoland*.

**Martin Jacques**
Economist and author of *When China Rules the World*
Many thanks for his contribution *Is China more legitimate than the West?*

**Catherine Chen** 陈小羽
Political analyst, Hangzhou China.

**Ian Johnson**
Writer, Pulitzer Prize winner
for his insights about religion in China

**Sean Ahluwalia,** BA Economics, MBA
For his contribution about the Chinese economy.

**Lawrence Trevethan**
China Political Analyst.

**The Rutherford Institute**
Non-profit organization based in Charlottesville, Virginia, US
dedicated to the defence of civil liberties.

**Zhāng Míng** 张明大使
Ambassador, Head of the Chinese Mission to the EU.

**Zhāng Cháoqún** 张张朝群
Former news editor at NRC Shanghai bureau.
For his honest testimony about the fraud at NRC in Shanghai.

**Richard A. Werner,**
"Princes of the Yen - Japan's Central Bankers and the Transformation
of the Economy", for his various recommendations and guidance.

**George Tait Edwards** PhD
for his contribution about *Shimomuran-Wernerian*
macroeconomic systems

**Shaun Lawson**
China analyst. International politics, science fiction, literature and
philosophy, cooking, as well as all things China

**Paul Denlinger**
*Hindsight, insight, foresight.* CEO, ChinaBridge Marketing Agency.
Publisher of *Reaching Chinese*, about marketing and advertising
globally and in China.
Curator of @ China's Future blog on Quora.

**Claire Cronshaw,** Copy editor.
For the careful and dedicated way in which she checked my
manuscript.

**Sūn Tóng** 孙彤
*Sint Lukas Design* made the beautiful design of the cover page

**Eswari Kamireddy,** Book layout designer

We'd like to credit all the original content providers. We have made
great efforts to provide sources of all reports, statistics, photos and
other data. For some texts and photos, we were unable to track down
the original source. Potential rights holders can turn to the publisher.

Beijing Tsinghua University Humanities and Social Sciences Library

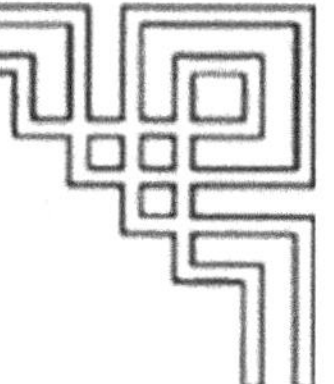



# About the Author, Accomplishments and Background.

*#author #background #accomplishments #photos #contact*

## Biography:

Frans Vandenbosch, Chinese name 方腾波, is a Fleming who lived in China for years. Previously, he has crossed all of China and visited more than 50 large and small towns and cities throughout the country.
During his professional activities in China, he supported companies in the automotive, medical, electronics and plastics processing sectors. He spent some time as a guest teacher at Qingdao University, was keynote speaker at conferences for Chinese entrepreneurs and gave interviews for Chinese business magazines.
As Technology Director at TGI, he has led the styling, design and engineering of new Chinese cars.
Cofounder and senior consultant at the International Institute on Governance and Strategy (IIGS)

Fig. 37 Frans Vandenbosch 方腾波 office in Shanghai

## Credentials, highlights, accomplishments:

Helping with rice harvest
in Chengyang, near to Guilin, 2002.

Lecture: Application of advanced
materials in automotive design.

Teaching Project Management
at Qingdao University.

Direction Technology at Tongji Innova
Chinese New Car Design. Shanghai.

Lecture: China Business at Marnixring.

Supporting Chinese students at
KULeuven University.

Chinese New Year Celebration
at KU Leuven
with Confucius Institute.

Writing for Dwarsliggers (sleeper/
naysayer) newsletter.

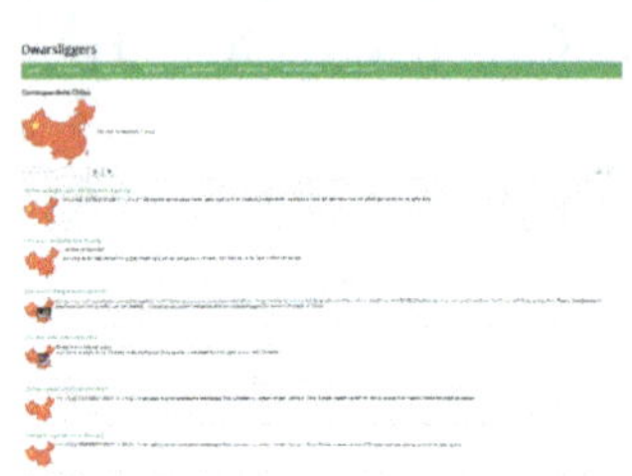

Assisting Chinese Automotive companies
Great Wall in Baoding, Hebei.

At the Sun Yat-Sen mausoleum
in Nanjing.

Managing Medical device manufacturing
Shanghai.

Reviewing EU-CN trade issues
at the Chinese EU mission (embassy)
in Brussels.

CCTV interview.

Plastic News China Magazine
interview.

At CNTV in Beijing.

Meeting with the China Culture
ambassador in Brussels.

The poem, **孙彤**Sūn Tóng my private teacher, wrote for me.

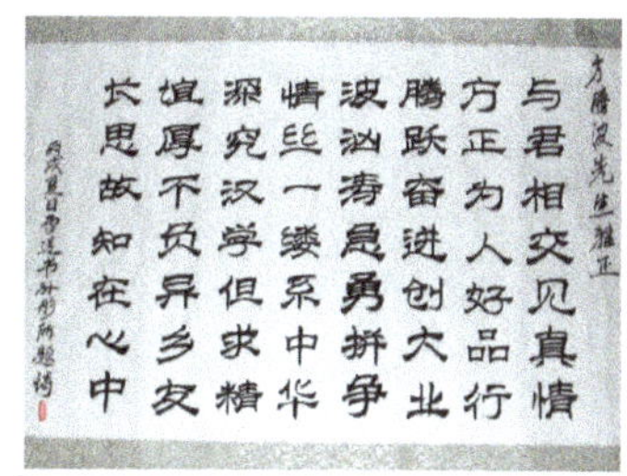

KU Leuven Alumni meeting in China.

Chinese language class
at KU Leuven university.

Art Exhibition in Shanghai.

With my first book about China.

Confucius Institute Leuven concert.

# Index.

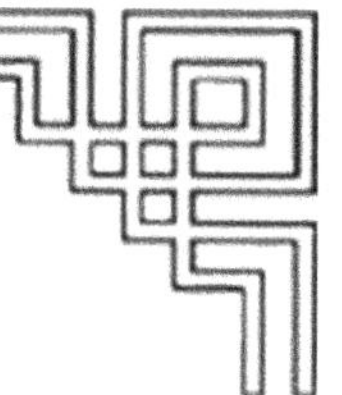

# Index

# S

Science and Civilisation in China  v
scientific basis  275
separation of powers  160, 161
service clubs  143
services  63, 73, 85, 162, 178, 179, 190,
    198, 199, 239, 240, 248, 249,
    251, 257, 258, 259, 262, 270,
    271, 273, 274, 275, 276, 280,
    286, 288, 289, 301
service standards  276
Serving the people  249
Shaanxi  126
Shanghai  43, 131, 132, 142, 168, 171,
    175, 177, 262, 302, 306, 307,
    309, 311
Shimomuran  71, 72, 73, 74, 77, 303
Shimomuran-Wernerian Macroeco-
    nomic  73
Sichuan  126, 193
Sina Weibo  109, 111
social autonomy  240
social cohesion  38, 197, 228, 231
social credit system  132
Social Credit System  10
socialism  76, 78, 81, 84, 87, 89
Socialism  49, 149, 234
Socialism with Chinese characteristics
    49
social management  234, 235, 236,
    237, 238, 239, 240, 241, 249,
    254, 255, 256, 276, 281, 282,
    287, 289, 300
social media  111, 160, 161, 186, 193,
    242
social mobility  237, 238
social organizations  111, 190, 238,
    239, 241, 256, 258
social services  190
social welfare  197, 199
society  2, 3, 4, 10, 13, 36, 43, 47, 48,
    105, 117, 129, 167, 174, 179,
    180, 181, 199, 227, 228, 230,
    231, 233, 234, 235, 236, 239,
    240, 241, 254, 255, 258, 259,
    261, 262, 280, 282, 294, 296
sociology  55
soft science  55
Song dynasty  72, 188, 280
South China Morning Post  137, 148
square dancing  130
stability  42, 88, 129, 179, 227, 228,
    229, 230, 231, 233, 235, 237,
    248, 250, 258, 262, 263, 264,
    276, 280, 281, 283
State Administration for Religious
    Affairs (SARA)  202
State Council  63, 65, 66, 67, 172, 195,
    202
Statecraft and Society in China  v
State-Owned Enterprises  76, 77
statistical analysis  270, 276
STEM graduates  55
stereotypes  49
stock exchange  77
Strategic Emerging Industries  76
students  55, 56, 109, 170, 176, 177,
    182, 293, 296
subsidiarity  47, 48
Supreme People's Court  64
Supreme Peoples Court  160, 162
Supreme Peoples Procuratorate  64
survey  85, 129, 131, 204, 264
Survey  23, 85, 264
Switzerland  16, 98

# T

taboo  108
technological developments  242
The Economist  14, 74
The New York Times  74
three ups and three downs  50
tiānmìng  62
Tiānxià  62
Tibet  136, 183, 229
training  156, 241, 250, 257

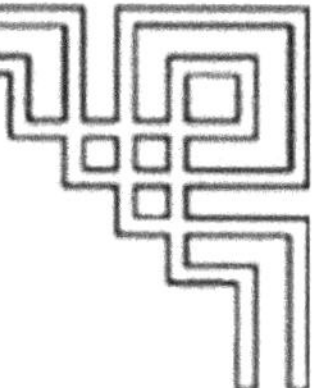



# 38.

# China Map.

*#China #map #administrative divisions*

*Fig. 38 China, Administrative Divisions.*

"This book depicts strong views, but is definitely not abrasive. Westerners who disagree will see this as biased, but it works both ways. They are biased too. It is certainly of great interest, especially to foreigners living in China and in other countries. I like the compact size of the chapters - not too long and involved."
**Edwin Maher, CCTV anchor.**

"Scientific accuracy, but written with passion and knowledge. I thoroughly enjoyed reading this as it is such an interesting topic"
**Claire Cronshaw.**

"Forget everything you have learned about China until you have read this book"
"To my knowledge, no other book reports in any detail about China at grassroots level. This book provides an altogether different picture of the heart of China, how ordinary people engage in politics"
**Richard Winnington.**

"I think your book is such a significant advance about grassroots politics in China that you should publish it as early as you can. In my judgement you have got the balance right. Best of luck with your book."
**George Tait Edwards.**

"I learned a lot of interesting details about the inner workings of the CPC's governance. 'Statecraft' shows how China's dynamic, participatory democracy directly benefits the people at the street level."
**Jeff J. Brown, Author of *The China Trilogy*.**

"I appreciate your vision and passion. Grassroots politics is indeed important for understanding China. And nicely designed and presented!"
*Robert Lawrence Kuhn.*